to Coordinator Schenck — for
better homes!

Geno Nelson

GEORGE NELSON · CONSULTANT EDITOR ARCHITECTURAL FORUM
HENRY WRIGHT · MANAGING EDITOR ARCHITECTURAL FORUM

TOMORROW'S HOUSE

HOW TO PLAN YOUR POST-WAR HOME NOW

SIMON AND SCHUSTER · NEW YORK 1945

ABOUT THE APPEARANCE OF BOOKS IN WARTIME

A ruling by the War Production Board has curtailed the use of
paper by book publishers. In line with this ruling and in order to
conserve materials and manpower, we are co-operating by:

1. Using lighter-weight paper, which reduces the bulk of our
books substantially.

2. Printing books with smaller margins and with more words to
each page. Result: fewer pages per book.

Slimmer and smaller books save paper and plate metal and labor.
We are sure that readers will understand the publishers' desire to
co-operate as fully as possible with the objectives of the War
Production Board and our government.

TABLE OF CONTENTS

FOREWORD
BY HOWARD MYERS · PUBLISHER OF ARCHITECTURAL FORUM

THIS IS NOT the first book about tomorrow's house. Nor will it be the last. But it is likely to be the most influential.

This book challenges not most, but all of the sweet-scented nostalgia on the domestic scene. Despite its persuasive manner, it is going to disturb many readers who keep their milk in the latest refrigerator, drive to business in the newest car, but persist in thinking that a Cape Cod cottage remains the snappiest idea in a home.

The thesis here advanced is that our way of life is undergoing great changes and that many of the changes are already here. If we accept that statement, and it would seem difficult not to, it follows that we should not let sentimental ties with the past stand in the way of getting the best house present-day technology and design can produce. The notion that the contemporary approach to design involves flat roofs and corner windows and the exclusion of rambler roses is one kind of nonsense this book aims to expose. Perhaps the greatest virtue of tomorrow's house is that it frees the plan—and therefore the family—from the arbitrary concepts which have gotten in the way of gracious living these many years.

Whether the talk is about windows or solar heat (of which you are hearing a lot now) or the living room, the authors have simplified their problems and yours by starting clean. They toss out completely the little partitioned cubicles called rooms and examine what goes on in a typical household—in short, how we live and how we want to live. Having established the ground rules, the book then proceeds to explain exactly how to get the kind of house which will permit us to live the kind of life we wish to live. And this seems the right place to quote Mr. Winston Churchill who not long ago said: "We shape our buildings, then our buildings shape our lives!"

I hope this book will be read by all those who plan to build or buy a postwar house. Obviously, they will be its greatest beneficiaries. But also, I have a special interest in seeing it read by those who make building their business. Every mortgage banker should read it to make certain the houses he finances will retain high resale value ten, fifteen, twenty years from now. Every house builder should read it if he aspires to greater success than his smug competitor. Every real estate man should read it because it can add a new note of conviction to his plea for home ownership—of the *right house*. And every architect should read it if only to stiffen his backbone when he tells the client, "You cannot walk backwards into the future!"

Finally, I must confess to a prejudice in favor of the authors. As one of their co-workers for nearly a decade. I have had abundant opportunity to observe how they think. Not only do they think regularly, but as a rule they think straight. Also, they have a persistent curiosity supported by professional training and skill which gives a basis to their opinions. Add to these personal qualities the job of conducting a building journal—they have bored into more house plans than any termites on earth—and Messrs. Nelson and Wright appear well equipped to handle the pages which follow.

In the first paragraph the opinion was ventured that this would be the most influential book on postwar houses. In essence what this book attempts to do is convince you that instead of "keeping up with the Joneses," it is more satisfying and profitable to be the "Joneses" under your own roof. If that prospect tempts you, here is the key.

ACKNOWLEDGMENTS

FEW BOOKS, and certainly no books of this type, appear without the silent but indispensable collaboration of many people. To these we gratefully acknowledge our considerable debt.

The fact that most of the words are spelled correctly is due to Eleanor Bittermann, Joanna Hadala and Rosamond Temple, who typed and retyped what seems in retrospect to have been an endlessly revised series of manuscripts.

The task of assembling photographs was carried through by Miss Henry Martin, who may also be held responsible for any errors in the lists of architects and photographers. That the pictures have been organized into a coherent group of illustrations is due to Paul Grotz, who designed the picture sections. It probably would have been impossible to have included even a fraction of the photographs if not for the pioneering work of *The Architectural Forum* in seeking out and publishing the best modern houses in America. The authors are grateful to both *The Forum* and *Life* for permission to show houses and projects previously published in these magazines.

To the rapidly expanding group of modern U.S. architects should go the bulk of the credit, since without their work there might have been theories to expound but no houses to demonstrate their validity.

The institution of matrimony exerted a very potent influence on the thinking of both authors in addition to the specific contributions made by Frances Nelson and Dorothy Wright, who carried through most of the research, deflated exaggerated ideas, corrected certain masculine misconceptions about the business of running a house, and edited the manuscript.

We gratefully acknowledge the cooperation of the photographers whose work appears in this volume. Their names are listed on page 214, together with the numbers of their photographs.

TOMORROW'S HOUSE

D

CHAPTER ONE

THE GREAT TRADITION

THIS BOOK HAS a point of view which may seem strange to you. What it is will be made pretty clear in the first few pages of this introduction. If, after reading that far, the viewpoint seems not only strange, but unpalatable as well, put this book aside and forget it, for what we have to say will not be for you.

We once knew a young couple who built a house.

They were an attractive, well educated, and prosperous pair. When their house—which they and their neighbors called "Colonial"—was completed, it was very impressive for its fine finish and generally beautiful workmanship. The delicate moldings characteristic of the style had been very carefully cut, and there were no rough edges anywhere. The builder who had put up this house had done a splendid job. But do you know what the owner and his wife did before the painters moved in? They went through all of the main rooms, each swinging a big bunch of heavy keys, banging away at the moldings which had been cut so carefully at the mill from the details prepared so carefully by the architect.

The moldings were nicked and scarred in this manner because it was felt that the house looked too new and therefore lacked the authenticity one finds in Salem or Litchfield or the other early New England towns.

If this little performance does not strike you as being pretty close to the lunatic fringe of human behavior, again we say: don't read this book.

Why do ostensibly normal young people, living in the twentieth century, do what this couple did to their new house?

Why do people buy new, straight beams for a study or living-room, and then hire a man with an adz to chip away at the surfaces until the beam looks as if it had been cut by a beaver instead of a modern sawmill?

Why do people spend money for shutters they never intend to use?

Why do most windows have eight to a dozen small panes, when single large sheets of glass are both cheaper and better? (Big, simple glass areas are much easier to clean, far easier to look out of.)

Why do people build houses that were designed originally to conform to the techniques and living requirements of people who were dead two hundred years ago? (The popular "Colonial" house is such a design.)

If we could discover the answers to these questions and others like them, we should be well on the way to discovering what a house today really is. You might say at this juncture, "But I do know what a house really is. It is a shelter for a family, so planned, constructed, and equipped that it gives the best possible accommodations for the money."

This is a very pretty definition. It might apply to

tomorrow's house. Unfortunately, it has practically nothing to do with today's.

There are three ways of looking at a house. A house is a technical fact—this is what the definition above is concerned with. But a house is also a social fact. And–something rarely thought of–it is a psychological fact of considerable importance. Only if we look at our homes in all three ways can we arrive at an answer to the question we started with.

HOME AS A TECHNICAL FACT

What is meant by the house as a technical fact? We use this phrase because a house, like any other product, is the result of design and production processes. Looked at in this way, home is no different from a pencil sharpener or a tractor. It shares with them the characteristic of being an item of consumer use. But there is one big difference, one, perhaps, which never occurred to you: our houses now represent the only important consumer product left that is still put together slowly, clumsily, and expensively, by hand. True, many of its parts are mass-produced in factories—thermostats, lighting and plumbing fixtures, refrigerators and hardware are not made on the job. By far the greater part, however, including the entire structural shell and foundations, is a pretty old-fashioned hand assembly. This is why homes cost so much. It isn't the only reason. But it is a big one.

Many people in the building business have been aware of this situation for years, and innumerable attempts have been made to design dwellings suitable for factory production. Most of these attempts come under the heading of "prefabrication," a word that has been very much in the limelight. To date, nobody has made a factory-built house that is more satisfactory than the conventional article and sells for less money. The time is not too far off, however, when such houses will be available. Ultimately they will represent the majority of new American dwellings.

2

Does this prospect bother you? If it does, let's not worry about it now. Prefabricated houses are not available, anyway. Our concern is with the house as it is built now and how to improve it.

When considering the house as a technical fact, it is well to remember that, while production methods are important, design methods at the present stage of building are even more important. Whether a home is hand- or machine-built, it is no good unless it is properly designed. "Design," by the way, means the basic scheme of the house, not just the trimmings around the front door and fireplace.

Today's house is a peculiarly lifeless affair. The picture one sees in residential neighborhoods the country over is one of drab uniformity: pathetic little white boxes with dressed-up street fronts, each striving for individuality through meaningless changes in detail or color. The reason today's house is so uninteresting is simply that it fails to echo life as we live it.

Expressed in another way, it is hideously inefficient. Less honest thought goes into the design of the average middle-class house than into the fender of a cheap automobile. Windows are placed with no regard for light or view. Rooms are arranged with little or no concern for their use and furnishings. Lighting, in a scientific sense, doesn't exist. Plans are so bad that nobody in the family can enjoy privacy outside of the bedroom or bath. Closets are usually the wrong size or shape, their doors make it hard to get full use out of them, and there are never enough. Except in the most up-to-date kitchens, few ideas have been developed for making housekeeping easier. Home may be the family's castle, but people got tired of living in castles several centuries ago.

HOME AS A SOCIAL FACT

If the house were just a collection of sticks and stones, working out an efficient design wouldn't be much of a job. Compared to a four-motored bomber or an aircraft carrier, a dwelling is a pretty simple affair. As it happens, however, home is a great deal more than a technical pattern: it is a member of society as well. And social patterns have been changing at a very rapid rate.

When families lived in small villages, when there were many children in each family, when people created their own entertainment in their own homes, lots of rooms were the rule. Efficiency, in our present-day sense, wasn't too important, because the tempo of life was slower and the children helped with the chores as they grew older. Also, there wasn't much the average housewife could do besides raising children and taking care of the home. Today this situation exists only in the most backward and isolated rural areas. Much entertainment has moved out of the home to the movies, to hotels, churches, night clubs, community houses, and other institutions which could hardly be said to have existed, in this sense, a generation ago. When the children grow up, they try to get jobs, they don't stick around to help with the dusting. Chances are that mother works too. It is difficult indeed to see how the conventional, old-style house can meet these new situations. In some places it has been decided that no kind of dwelling can meet all of them. This last statement probably needs amplification.

In Stockholm there are thousands of apartment dwellings constructed by co-operative building societies for their members. Many of the buildings, which run to about eight stories high, have penthouses and large roof gardens. These penthouses and gardens are not for wealthy tenants: they are set aside for the children of all the tenants. They contain nurseries which are beautifully equipped and capably staffed. There are kitchens, examining rooms, sunny playrooms, dormitories, and small isolation wards. The nurseries are used in a great variety of ways. If both parents work, the child is taken up in the morning to spend the day in the nursery, and collected again in the evening. Should the mother stay at home, the child may only spend enough time in the nursery to allow the mother to get her cleaning and marketing done. If the parents feel they need a week-end alone together, there are dormitories where the children can sleep and kitchens for feeding them. If someone in the family is ill, the children can be moved to the nursery for protection. The net result of this system, which has been extraordinarily successful in Sweden, is that families in the $1,500 to $3,000 income group have more freedom in their daily lives than many people here whose incomes may be five times as great.

There are two conclusions which may be drawn from this example. One is that there are certain functions which no home, however modern and efficient, can provide. Such problems can only be solved by social action, by groups that pool their requirements and their resources. The second conclusion, which follows inevitably, is that whenever certain home functions are taken over by agencies outside the home, the plan of the dwelling itself can be modified.

It is not within the province of this book to argue for or against nurseries. The example is cited only to illustrate the contention that many traditional home activities are moving out into the neighborhood or the community. Under the circumstances, therefore, the influence of this trend, as well as others—say factory work for women—must be considered in its relation to the individual dwelling.

Not all social trends are on this grand scale. The phenomenal growth of hobbies is another one. Hobbies are a peculiarly modern activity. They are partly the result of increased leisure, partly an attempt to compensate for the spiritual poverty of life in an overspecialized world. Wherever a hobby requires space—say photography or woodworking—the plan of the house must be modified. There are many similar examples of social pressures which tend to change the form of the house.

HOME IS A PSYCHOLOGICAL FACT

Hardest to evaluate of all three aspects of today's house is what we have termed the psychological. When a man buys a car it would scarcely be accurate to say that his emotions are deeply involved in the transaction. For one thing, he has no intention of keeping the car for more than three to five years. For another, it is primarily a means of transportation. True, people do become fond of their cars and their idiosyncrasies, and they get a great deal of pleasure from the freedom of movement a car offers, but there is rarely much anguish when the jalopy is traded in for a shiny new model. Home is quite a different matter.

Did you ever hear of a "Dream Car"? We haven't. But there is an American "Dream House," and all of us have been conditioned to want it. This dream house has become so standardized that we can even describe it.

Home, in the American dream, is a quaint little white cottage, shyly nestled in a grove of old elms or maples, bathed in the perfume of lilacs, and equipped with at least one vine-covered wall. Its steep gabled roof, covered with rough, charmingly weathered shingles, shows a slight sag in the ridge. The eaves come down so low that one can almost touch them. Tiny dormers on one side poke themselves through the old roof and let in light through tiny-paned windows to the upstairs bedrooms. In front of the house there is invariably a picket fence, with day lillies poking their heads between the white palings. Let into the fence, at the end of a flagstone walk bordered with alyssum and verbena, is a swinging gate, where husband and wife embrace tenderly as he dashes for the 8:11 and the workaday world. Finishing touches include shutters in soft blue or green, with half moons or flower pots cut out of them with a jig saw. In the hall there is a replica of an oil lamp, wired for electricity. Somewhere there is a paneled wall, a beamed ceiling, a hooked rug, a four-poster bed, and a huge

4

fireplace of worn old brick with an antique settle or shoemaker's bench in front of it.

"Well," you may say, "what's wrong with that picture? It looks pretty good to me."

There is nothing wrong with the picture—except that it remains what it always was, a dream. No house embodying all of these features ever existed at any one time or place. When people attempt to realize it today, what they actually get is either a cheap imitation or an outrageously expensive fake. And in the end the whole thing is given away by the late model Buick at the front door (which requires a very untraditional driveway and garage), or by the kitchen ventilating fan, or a television aerial, not to mention the tiled bath and streamlined kitchen. People refuse to live in the seventeenth century even though they sometimes like to pretend that is what they are doing.

To approach the biggest investment in a family's life in such peculiarly sentimental terms seems irrational, to say the least. At such a time we should be thinking very hard about getting the very best living features for the money; instead, we dream of a kind of house that was developed before we finished fighting the Indians.

There is something else about this dream house which is odd. The picture is not "traditional"— that is, it does not go back without interruption to pioneer days. After the Civil War, during the Victorian period, people didn't think in these terms at all. The Victorian house, for example, was a surprisingly uninhibited design and very functional in a good many ways. It was quite sensibly related to the techniques and living habits of the period. Queer as their tastes may have been, the people of this time felt no compulsion, apparently, to squeeze themselves into counterfeit Cape Cod cottages. The Colonial dream with which we have all been obsessed goes back only to the time of World War I. Why?

The end of World War I opened one of the most

chaotic periods in human history. One year and four days before the armistice was signed, the Russians under Lenin inaugurated a social and economic system, the implications of which have never ceased to frighten people whose well-being depends on the ownership of productive property. After the German people had swapped the Kaiser for the Weimar Republic, they headed into a period of disastrous inflation. Trying to establish a government on the Bolshevik model, the North Italian workers precipitated the crisis that brought in Mussolini and Fascism. The wildest boom ever known came to a sudden end in 1929, and tens of millions of people the world over suddenly found themselves helpless and jobless. Full-scale wars have been raging in Asia, Africa, and Europe since 1931. These events, tossed into the lap of a generation born in the smug, quiet years which began the century, were profoundly distressing, because the forces generating the events were hard to understand and seemingly impossible to control.

World War I had another consequence. It opened the eyes of industrialists to the meaning of full-scale mass production. Factories sprang up by the thousands, and markets were flooded with countless items that were lower in price and higher in quality than any consumer goods ever produced before. Thus, before the eyes of a new generation, another contradiction presented itself: production potential without limit on the one hand: unemployment without limit on the other. Alone in a world that made little sense and offered less security, the average citizen searched desperately for ways out of the dilemmas into which he was continually being placed. Never in his whole history had he been so free. He was "free" to work—if he could find work. He was "free" to buy anything—if he had money. He was "free" to move anywhere he wanted—if there was a job at the other end. He had other kinds of freedom, too. Good kinds. But for the most part he was like a chip tossed around

in a strong current, and of this kind of freedom he was terrified.

When people become afraid of freedom, they try to give it up. They regiment themselves, because regimentation provides a comforting sense of security, of belonging to something. The comfort doesn't last, but people try it anyway.

We know how regimentation worked in Germany and Italy. In our own country it is less blatant, because what we are destroying is cultural, not political, freedom. Every week tens of millions of people rush to the movies, where the usual film preaches that there is no need to worry—there is always a happy ending. Let the czars of fashion announce that skirts are going to be an inch higher or lower, and female America trots off docilely to obey. Fear is the keynote of smart advertising: we buy because we are afraid of B.O. or halitosis or losing a girl—never because we like the stuff. Over a million people belong to "clubs" which tell them what books to buy. Then they buy digests so that they won't have to read the books. Expose someone to a strange new painting or unfamiliar music, and ask for a reaction. Usually what you get is an evasion. Modern man, put into a spot where he can't function on canned opinion, tends to get lost. He has no confidence in his taste or judgment. He is regimented.

And so with our houses. For a while the rage was "Mediterranean." Later it was "English" and "French Provincial." Most recently it has been "Colonial." The names of the styles don't matter, because most of the houses have been very poor imitations, anyway. But what did that matter? All that really mattered was not getting out of step with the crowd.

The "Dream House" exists because to the person who has lost his capacity for independent thinking and feeling it represents authority, expert opinion, tradition, and cultural solidarity with his fellows. Also, it subtly identifies its owner with people who weren't afraid to think and feel for themselves, with a time when families moved boldly into the uncharted wilderness because they knew what they were after. Armed with a dream house, the bewildered citizen thinks he has one thing at least which will stay put in a changing world, a link to the past which suggests, but does not really provide, security. This house has the magic property of making one just like everyone else. It is not "extreme" or "freakish." Its features have been made known to every man and woman in the land through the women's magazines, the home magazines, movies, and advertisements. It is, therefore, respectable. For this respectability the buyer pays a high price, because he sacrifices all kinds of living amenities in the process.

WHAT IS A HOUSE?

Now it is clear why our young friends banged up their moldings. The old-fashioned design was not enough—the house had to show the very scars of long usage. We all want safety, permanence, continuity. But what a strange way to try to get them! Now it is also clear why the shutters, the fake beams, and all the other stage scenery are put in. We can see, too, why modern houses were greeted at the outset with such violent outbursts of disapproval. "Modern" was more than a way of designing houses—it was one more symbol of incomprehensible change. And every change, these days, seems to be a threat to personal and social stability.

What is a house? We now have an answer. It is a perfect mirror of a society most of whose members are desperately afraid of acting like independent individuals. Its weaknesses are social, not technical. The technical means for producing good houses have long been at hand. Today's house is the crudest kind of solution to the problem of gracious, civilized living; it is decades behind the industrial possibilities of our time. Tomorrow's house—the

antithesis of everything we have said about today's —could be built right now by anyone who has the good sense and courage to tackle it.

A LOOK AT MODERN

If you have already glanced at the pictures in this book, you will have noticed that there are no examples of the Colonial Dream House. Interiors, exteriors, furnishings, and equipment are all modern. In other words, they were built by people who haven't been afraid to change. To date, such people have put up enough modern houses to fill several books this size. In the next five years or so, dozens of times as many are going to be built. The Colonial dream is approaching its end. How do we know? In two ways. We have been watching the advertisements, the movies, and the magazines, and the swing to modern has definitely begun. All of our tremendous apparatus for influencing public opinion is tuning up for a new propaganda barrage in favor of these new houses. A new fashion in homes will be created, and the public will follow. There is another reason for this prediction, a far more important one. People have been learning that the houses they have been sold are not good enough. Where they have seen good modern houses, they have been impressed. They know living in a house can be better than it has been, and they are beginning to make their demands felt.

At this point one thing has to be made very clear, for it is the basis on which the entire book has been written. *We are in favor of modern houses, not because they are modern, but because they are traditional.* This undoubtedly sounds strange enough to require an explanation. Here it is:

Whenever people run across buildings which history books say are great architecture, we find that these buildings have certain characteristics in common. Invariably they were unself-conscious and honest solutions to some particular set of building problems. Their architects were men who worked

6

right now the means to create homes of designs so advanced that they would be able to meet every requirement of contemporary living.

Mind you, we don't expect anyone to go through this process of tossing all the best things into a hat and pulling out the perfect house. Things don't happen that way. Tomorrow's house as we see it is not a potpourri but an integrated, highly individual expression of how a twentieth-century family lives. And to get that you need a family that knows what it needs and has the courage of its convictions. You also need an architect worth his salt. Both are to be found, but there is no oversupply of either.

THIS BOOK

The statement of our thesis should help to explain the organization of the material in the book. You will find no stock plans here, no catalogues of "styles," no orations on good taste. You will run across many detailed solutions for general problems, but much more about how to solve your own. The photographs and drawings were not put in to be copied, although if you find a good idea suitable for your own requirements, by all means take it. They will be far more useful, however, if they are studied for what they achieve, and analyzed to find how they got that way.

Anyone who has followed articles on houses in the popular magazines and has watched recent advertisements is conscious of the tremendous interest in new materials and gadgets, things which promise to make tomorrow's house a revolutionary affair in many ways. If this is what you expect of this book—detailed specifications of things to come—you will be sadly disappointed. There is very little here about miraculous things to come, but a great deal about miraculous things that have been with us for some time. The relative absence of glamorous descriptions of new wonder plastics, light metals yet to be named, and electronic equip-

ment that will change the baby's diapers, is not due to a lack of interest on our part. But in combing through the technical papers, in tracking down promising announcements, and by utilizing every possible contact with specialists in the building industry, we were forced to the conclusion that the *immediate* future holds little in the way of epoch-making developments that will have any significant influence on home design. This does not mean that important changes are not in the offing—in the chapter called "Projections" there are indications of many. These, however, will not vitally affect tomorrow's house; they are for the day after tomorrow at the earliest. And interesting as they are as trends today, it will be years before they have any practical meaning for the home builder.

Wherever possible, the "functional" approach has been used, not because this is the be-all and end-all of house design, but because it is a good way to begin. You will not find a chapter on bedrooms, for example, but a great deal about sleeping. If people are going to sleep, it doesn't much matter whether they do it on the couch in the living room or on a bed in the bedroom; in both places the requirements are exactly the same. It may come as a surprise that certain rooms have been so dealt with that they have turned into completely different kinds of rooms. In place of the conventional kitchen, for instance, we give you the "work center," which is not merely a new label but a new kind of interior. Perhaps you won't like it. If so, that is all right with us. It is definitely not the purpose of this book to *dictate* a new gospel of house planning. It has been enough of a job to explore some of the myriad possibilities offered by contemporary living habits and industrial techniques and to show some of the ways they can be used to make houses better, more attractive places to live. If you are interested in this objective (and who is not?), we think you will find the book provocative and, we hope, useful and convincing.

CHAPTER TWO

Hearty

HOME IS WHERE YOU

HANG YOUR ARCHITECT

If He doesn't Give you what you Want

THIS IS NOT a true story, but it might just as well be.

Once upon a time there was a Man who decided that he would build a house for his family and himself. Before calling in the architect he had selected, he himself started to work out a plan for the house, because, he reasoned, he knew more about his family and how it functioned and what it liked and what it didn't like and what it could afford and what their friends didn't like, than anybody else.

He began with the living-room, because, after all, he only slept in the bedroom and never went into the kitchen.

His plan for the living-room was really pretty wonderful. There had been very few living-rooms, probably, with as many masculine comforts included. There was, for instance, a place for his favorite leather chair, which was well worn and comfortable. And there was a good floor lamp with a bright bulb arranged so that one could read without shifting around in the chair, moving the lamp, and otherwise wasting a great deal of time and comfort.

Within arm's reach on one side was the radio. On the other there was a smoking stand with room for magazines, a couple of books, a jar of tobacco, and four or five pipes.

One side of the room was to be lined with

books, because the Man liked to read. And there was even a cabinet which when opened up would turn into the most ingenious bar imaginable.

When the plan was done, the Man showed it to his wife. "This" he said, "is the plan of the living-room in our new house. Isn't it wonderful? Look."

"No," said his wife, "it isn't wonderful at all. In fact, I'd hardly call it a living-room. It looks more like the extra bedroom upstairs that you wanted so that you could have a quiet place."

"Why, what do you mean?" sputtered the Man. "Now, look—"

"A living-room," interrupted his wife icily, "is called a living-room because other people in the

Father's plan

10

family will have to live in it besides you. When my friends come in for bridge, what good will that ratty old leather chair of yours do them? And I'm not sure I will even allow that in our new house, anyway. Don't forget that I am chairman of two committees, one of which has sixteen members, and when they come to the house, as they will have to do at least once a month, I must have room for them. And if we have tea we are going to need tables. Besides, what will people think if instead of a decent living-room we have this smoke-filled den you seem bent on acquiring!"

"Well, maybe you have a point there," said the husband, who always ended up by agreeing his wife had a point there. "What had we better do? I've wanted a decent place to read, you know, for quite a long time, and this seemed like a good chance to get it. You're not going to spoil my corner, are you?"

"Certainly not," said the wife, who was much more cheerful now that matters were obviously under control and moving in the right direction. "Of course not. After a long, hard day at the office you need a nice place where you can read in comfort. But about the living-room. I saw the most attractive picture in *House and Home* last month. It had a charming fireplace with some really stunning

eighteenth century French andirons. And right in front of the fireplace there was an antique coffee table with a sofa on each side. Then behind one sofa there was a high table with a pair of very handsome Chinese lamps on it."

At this point their daughter, who had walked in on the discussion a few minutes earlier and had evidenced mounting indignation, burst in.

"I never heard anything so ridiculous in all my life! Isn't there going to be any place in this house where your children can carry on a normal social life? Why, anybody would think you didn't have any children or didn't care about them. Why don't you build us a separate house?"

The Man and his wife, having weathered these outbursts for a good part of the last sixteen years, regarded their daughter with their usual mixture of affection and perplexity, tacitly dropping their own argument to join forces against the forthcoming attack.

"A living-room," continued their daughter indignantly, "is a place where the family should live, isn't it? Why do you have to dress it up like a third-rate interior decorator's dream of life in a penthouse? Do you have to clutter up the room with that heavy table and those two Chinese lamps? I know what you're talking about. We saw it in

Mother's Living Room

Roan's window when we were downtown day before yesterday. Now, I ask you! How do we ever move that out of the way if we're having a party and someone wants to dance? And with those two chi-chi sofas so close to the fireplace, how would anybody ever get in there to make popcorn or toast marshmallows? What's more, if a girl wanted to entertain somebody—just one person, I mean—she would have about as much privacy as a—a—."

"Goldfish," suggested her father helpfully.

In the brief silence that followed, many thoughts were whirling around in the minds of the living-room planners.

"Guess I lose my reading corner," thought the Man.

"I don't suppose I'll ever have a really nice living-room," thought his wife, "and I've wanted one for so long."

"Why don't they ever do things right," fretted the daughter. "Does a girl have to wait until she's married to get a nice place to live?"

Habit was strong, however. But with the first move towards compromise, in walked son John, age fourteen, whose passion for swing bands had turned the dinner hour into a silent, recurring battle over whether he or his father would get to the radio first when dessert was cleared away. And the three suddenly realized that this was the most difficult factor of all—John and his drums and his three music-loving companions who weekly made the neighborhood air quiver with their uneasy efforts to achieve something new in contemporary music.

Late that night the discussion continued in the privacy of the master bedroom.

"—And you see, my dear," continued the wife, decisively snapping her hair net into place, "there also has to be at least one decent place where I can work. There's all the mending, which means some kind of cabinet in the living-room, because it's silly to run up and down with a sewing basket, and a good strong light. And we need a desk, because we have to keep bills and household accounts and write letters somewhere."

Overwhelmed by the seemingly endless list of requirements, the Man grunted and fell asleep. So, eventually, did his wife. And her consciousness of the requirements and desires of the rest of her family must have penetrated her subconscious, for she drifted presently into a dream of Bessie, an irate Bessie, the maid they had had the longest time and a family member they were most anxious to keep.

"I quit!" Bessie was saying over and over again in the dream. "I can't clean that living-room! You

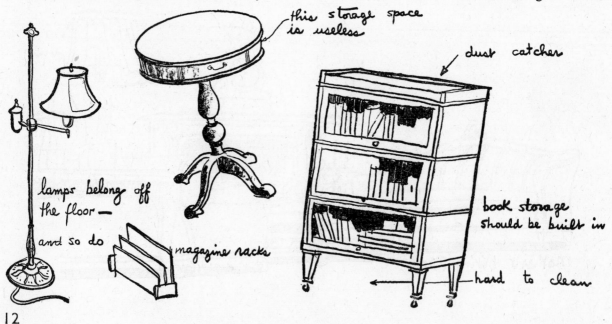

this storage space is useless

dust catcher

lamps belong off the floor—

and so do magazine racks

book storage should be built in

hard to clean

should have one servant just to work there and no-where else. I can't get the vacuum cleaner under those spindle-legged sofas, so I have to move them. But you can't move them, because there are tables on both sides. So I move the tables. But you can't move the tables, because they're too heavy. Then there's that corner of yours. No matter what I do to that old leather chair, it never looks right. And there are the cigar ashes on that beautiful new rug. Master John won't let me move his drums, and I can't clean around them or under them. And Miss Peggy's friends got toasted marshmallow all over one of the upholstered chairs last night. I can hardly move around, because you've got three floor lamps now.

"I quit!" screamed Bessie, vanishing into a black void where the wife could not even find a fragment of pride in working out a living-room that would make everybody in the family happy.

Breakfast the following day was better. Planning was in the air. Each member of the family sensed in his or her own way the challenge and excitement of arranging things so that this room would do every-thing that they demanded of it. They were all gen-uinely fond of one another, and the bickering was almost always amiable.

"Let's make a list," said the mother.

A list was made forthwith. Or, rather, four lists were made.

Putting them together was the most fascinating game of give-and-take the family had ever played. But as the room emerged from this building-up of requirements, it took on a rather curious and dis-turbing quality, for it was not like any room any of them could recall having seen before.

There were, for example, thirteen different sources of light. Some were high and some were low, some were dim and some were bright, some were direct and some were indirect. They had never seen a room with thirteen lights in it before, but the idea seemed to make sense. And, anyway, they had gotten rid of the three floor lamps, because nobody liked floor lamps. There was even to be a funny black spotlight, screwed on the wood wall in the alcove, just like the ones in the show windows down at Lloyd's. But they had mulled over the question of lights, and this they knew was what they needed.

There was acoustical tile on one wall—just as there was in Dad's office—to counteract some of the effects of the swing band. And there was one wall that seemed to be mostly glass, which could be made to slide so that in summer the porch would become part of the living-room, and everybody

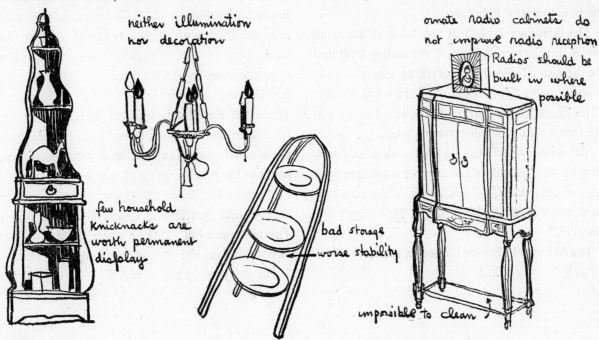

neither illumination nor decoration

few household knicknacks are worth permanent display

bad storage worse stability

ornate radio cabinets do not improve radio reception
Radios should be built in where possible

impossible to clean

The local courthouse

would have more space.

At this point they went to their Architect, who was a very distinguished old gentleman. He had built the local courthouse, a very fine Italian Renaissance building. The main lobby had a wonderful corridor with a ceiling you would have sworn was made out of wood beams. Everybody in town knew they were concrete, of course, but nobody had ever seen so good an imitation. He had done houses in the best sections of town—stately Georgian mansions, the most intimate kind of French farmhouses, and even a Mediterranean villa, which looked too tropical for words, except, of course, in the worst part of February.

The Architect looked at the list and heard all about the thirteen lights and the sliding wall and the acoustical tile and everything else that was needed for the living-room. And the slight wrinkle in his distinguished forehead broadened into a polite frown that gradually became fixed.

"It's impossible," he said finally, delicately tapping his gold pencil on the top of his antique desk (one of the finest Chinese Chippendale pieces ever produced west of the Mississippi). "It's simply impossible."

The Man and his wife looked at each other.

"Why?" they asked.

"Because," said the Architect, "there has never at any period, in any style, been the kind of living-room you are talking about. If you should build this astonishing creation, it would have no Proportion, Symmetry, or Style. In fact, it would have no architectural quality of any kind. It would be incorrect. It would be bad form. You would become a laughing stock. And I cannot allow any of these things to happen to any of my clients."

The Man and his wife were silent and subdued. How had they managed to break so many rules? All they had wanted was a living-room.

"Well," said the Man finally, "I can see that we should have come to an expert in the first place. You had better go ahead and show us what we should have in our living-room."

Gratified, the Great Architect smiled benignly and reached behind him for the well-thumbed copies of *Stately Homes of the English Aristocracy of the Early Eighteenth Century* by Marmaduke Chilblane, and *Country Houses of the Borgias, Illustrated with Photographs and Detail Drawings*, by Baron Occhio di Porco, and *Rooms Louis XIV Was Particularly Fond Of* by Lady Meddle. The Great Architect was ready to design another house.

The ending of this story is very sad or very beautiful, depending on how you look at it. The thirteen lights were replaced by four very chaste gold-and-antiqued-mirror wall brackets and two lamps that easily gave enough light so that nobody stumbled over the long-legged little tables that were scattered all over the fine imitation Aubusson carpet. When the house was finished, the Man did his reading in the bedroom, his wife did her sewing in the kitchen, their daughter took over the rumpus room in the basement (which was built as an afterthought and in sheer desperation), and the swing band found quarters in somebody else's house. This last was admitted to be a very successful piece of planning on the part of the Great Architect.

The story might have had a different ending, but

the Man and his wife did not find this out until many years after the house was built. By then they had become so accustomed to the dreary correctness of their house and its living-room, and had so adapted themselves to its manifold inconveniences, that they forgot about the living-room that was designed for living rather than the gratification of a Great Architect, the home magazines, and the most sheeplike of their friends.

But many other people did not forget. There had already begun to appear in Switzerland and Sweden and Holland and France, in San Francisco and Spring Green, Wisconsin; in New York, Chicago, and other places, architects and designers who were not shocked by the idea of thirteen lights in one room or sliding walls or old leather chairs.

To these people it seemed perfectly natural to design a room for those who were going to use it. A room was a space created by walls of some sort and a floor and a ceiling, so fitted with equipment and furniture that you could do exactly what you wanted in it in the way you wanted to do it.

One of these architects even made a proclamation about it in the early days. "A house," he said, "is a machine for living in."

The people who came later thought that even this declaration cramped their style. And they began to forget about the "machine" as an end in itself and to think more about what it could do for better living.

CHAPTER THREE

HOW TO PLAN A LIVING-ROOM

FIRST, WE DO exactly what the family in the last chapter did. We make lists. Certain activities will cancel each other out. For example, writing letters, doing homework, settling the household accounts, and various other occupations can all be taken care of at a good desk. To be sure, there will be occasions when one desk will prove inadequate. Someone will want to write letters at the same time someone else wants to do homework. If such situations are likely to arise very often, planning takes this into account by providing a secondary desk. This might be the dining-room table or even a table in the kitchen. Possibly it will be decided that homework will not be done in the living-room at all, but in the bedroom, and a space there will be planned for it.

NOISE

Some of these overlapping requirements may have fairly elaborate solutions. But it is both good fun and real economy to do this kind of multiple planning wherever possible. For example, it is being recognized that acoustical treatment has almost as important a role to play in the house as it has had in offices and moving-picture theaters. As it happens, a wall of books has certain acoustical properties. It does not reflect sound as readily as a smooth wood or plaster wall. Book covers are soft and tend to absorb some of the sound. So do the cracks between the books and the spaces above them. Libraries, you know, are traditionally quiet places, and many of us have thought that it was because everyone took care not to make any noise. Actually, however, the existence of walls lined with books constitutes an excellent sound-deadening treatment. The atmosphere of quiet in many libraries is due as much to the books themselves as to the considerate behavior of the people reading them. Here we have a real tool in planning a living-room—provided, of course, that there is a desire to absorb sound and make the room quieter, and provided, also, that one happens to own a lot of books. If both of these conditions obtain, and in a great many families they do, we have a method of absorbing sound that won't cost a cent, because the books have to go somewhere, anyway.

This is just one example of dozens which might be listed.

If acoustical treatment is to some extent expenditure of money and to a larger extent a matter of using one's head, the same is more true of lighting. Lighting in the average home is so important, and it has been so badly handled to date, that we have devoted an entire chapter to it. This much, however, might be said here.

LIGHT

In the living-room more than in any other room, flexibility of lighting is exceedingly desirable. The room should be bright on some occasions, dim on others. It should have many special installations designed to make reading, sewing, and other activities as easy on the eyes as possible, and at the same time it should not become so cluttered with fixtures—either table or floor lamps—that cleaning and moving around become inconvenient.

The problem of providing light where it is wanted, and in the proper quantity and quality, cannot be solved with conventional home fixtures. For this reason many architects have turned to the equipment produced for commercial and industrial rather than domestic use. They are already producing home lighting of high quality and flexibility. (In this book you will find that a great deal will be said about flexibility.)

FLEXIBILITY

Consider, for example, the initial disagreements of our family when they began to plan their living-room. Much of the argument revolved around questions of seating. Father wanted his comfortable old leather chair next to the radio. Mother wanted couches and chairs for committee meetings, bridge, and entertaining her friends. Daughter wanted seating facilities, too, but of a different kind. On many occasions, although they didn't talk about it, the family wanted practically no seating at all— just one or two chairs where one or two people might sit quietly and read or talk or listen to music without feeling that the room looked too big or too barren.

Here is a real problem for the planner. How do you design a room so that it looks warm and intimate with two people in it, but never overcrowded with thirty? In a way it sounds like an insoluble problem, unless one assumes that the living-room is to be made out of rubber and stretched on appropriate occasions.

The problem, however, is not insoluble. But to find the answer—or, rather, the answers, for there are several solutions—it is necessary to look at this aspect of living-room design with something of a fresh viewpoint.

As we sit here working on this chapter, we are looking at two photographs of living-rooms. Both are in houses designed by Frank Lloyd Wright. One is a very large room; it must be thirty or forty feet square. It is the main room in his country house, Taliesen, which was built not far from Spring Green, Wisconsin. The other is in a much more modest residence in a Chicago suburb.

In the smaller living-room, which looks as if it could take care of a cocktail party for two dozen people, there is not a single visible piece of movable furniture, with the unimportant exception of a small coffee table in front of the fireplace. There is, however, a couch built in under convenient bookshelves and cabinets which is large enough to stretch out on, or to seat six or eight people. There are several counters and tables, built against the walls, providing very attractive practical surfaces on which to put books, meals, flowers, or anything else. In the particular photograph we have, it is also interesting to see that there are no lamps sitting around, because the architect built his lighting fixtures into the ceiling, and all that shows is a flush rectangle of frosted glass.

In the big living-room at Taliesen, this use of built-in living equipment is even more remarkable. Here, in a small alcove, one can sit all alone in the evening by the fire and feel quite comfortable. And the same room functions equally well with as many as fifty or sixty people. The secret of this remarkable flexibility is again to be found in the use of built-in seating, which is always so inconspicuous that it seems like a part of the room's architecture. Yet, when a crowd turns up, it is always available for people to sit on.

17

The peaceful atmosphere of such rooms as these must be experienced to be fully understood. But the basic idea, that the room itself provide seating and table top space rather than accomplishing these functions with furniture moved in after the room is done, is of great importance. It is also important to note that in such rooms the essential equipment is provided *at the walls*. The center is free. It can be left clear or chairs and light tables can be moved in as they are needed. This is part of what is meant when we talk of flexibility.

How many of the living-rooms with which you are acquainted are too cluttered? If any of us were honest about our own houses and those of our friends, we would be forced to agree that half or more of the furniture which gets in one's way could well be eliminated and replaced by less expensive, less conspicuous, built-in units, and that a great deal of the junk lying around on bookshelves, table tops, and so on, could be thrown out or at least put in cabinets where it would be out of the way.

STORAGE

The old idea of the living-room never included a closet. Nor was storage space of any kind considered essential. There might be a table with two or three drawers in it, which would be jammed with playing cards, seed catalogues, letters, canceled checks, and dozens of other odds and ends. But this could hardly be considered storage.

Phonograph records, for instance, need to be kept safely out of sight, away from dust. There is no need to mess up the room with them. The same is true of game equipment—chess and backgammon boards, bridge tables, poker chips, score pads, and the like. And there are always the extra ash trays, cartons of cigarettes, coasters for glasses, and all the other paraphernalia of entertainment.

This, incidentally, provides one of the major con-

These need living room space for storage.

18

trasts between the living-room in the modern house, which invariably has one or several cabinets filled with shelves, drawers, and compartments, and the conventional type of interior where nothing of the sort is provided.

Attention to storage units as a factor in providing greater flexibility for living also has a profound effect on the housewife's problems of keeping the place in order. There is a house in one of New York's suburbs, for instance, with a living-room supplied with forty-five running feet of storage cabinets. These extend the full length of one wall and out into the hall. The whole house, in fact, is equipped with all sorts of storage units in addition to the usual closets, and one result, according to the owners, has been a great saving in time and energy and money.

Originally it was believed three servants would be needed to keep the house in order. When the family moved in, it was found that two did the job very well—a saving which paid for all of the extra units (in a few years, it might be added). Then, when the war came and servants disappeared, the family found that it could run the house under its own steam without too much difficulty.

"Clutter" can mean a great many things. In many of Frank Lloyd Wright's houses the floors are of brick or polished concrete. In some cases the rugs have been omitted entirely. This might sound like an exchange of comfort for ease in cleaning, and most people would prefer the comfort. However, these houses are radiant-heated through warm water pipes embedded in the concrete floor slab. The major source of discomfort with this kind of floor—its coldness—has consequently been eliminated.

This does not mean, of course, that rugs should be discarded. It simply suggests that they can be, if for any reason the owner feels that it would be desirable or more economical.

Pictures on the wall are another, and a particularly irritating, way of cluttering up interiors. The pictures in most houses are so appallingly ugly or commonplace that it is impossible to understand how they got there in the first place. They have long since ceased to be objects providing any enjoyment for the family or its friends, but nobody dares to get rid of them because of the marks they would leave on the wall and because the room would look so "bare" without them.

The argument here is not against pictures—if they are pictures one can look at with honest enjoyment—but against the misunderstanding of the essential purpose of a picture and its proper use.

A picture is not a decoration. It represents in a limited area some experience an artist has had, which, when communicated to other people, gives them a certain amount of pleasure and a better understanding of the world around them. In this sense a picture is not entirely unlike a book. But who would sit and read the same book over and over and over again day in and year out? The only known example—the hypothetical castaway on the imaginary desert island with the ten best books—is the closest approximation to date, and who would want to be in his spot?

It is true that decorators will frequently "build a room" around some picture. They will set a print of a masterpiece—for instance, a Van Gogh landscape—over the fireplace and take the yellows and greens and blues and earth red and repeat these colors in the curtains, upholstery fabrics, wall paint or covering, and so on. The result is proclaimed to be an artistic and harmonious job where picture and room become a unified whole. Actually, it is the cheapest trick imaginable for borrowing some of the respectability of an acknowledged work of art for the purpose of making a decorating job look more impressive.

Keying a room to a picture would be a good idea if one didn't get tired of the picture. But anyone with eyes in his head and a minimum of honesty

19

must confess that any picture, however fine, becomes very boring if looked at for very long. The reason most of us do not get impatient with the pictures in our houses is that we have long since ceased to look at them.

The solution here is again provision for flexibility. One of the storage cabinets whose uses we have just been considering could perfectly well hold a dozen or a hundred favorite pictures. Whether they are originals or reproductions, incidentally, doesn't matter a bit, except to those snobs who are unable to appreciate art except in terms of how much it costs. The reproductions on the market today, so many of which are the same size as the original and very faithful in their rendering of color and even of texture, are just as good from the viewpoint of the average man as the originals. This is indicated clearly enough by the fact that you can't tell half the time whether you are looking at an original or reproduction until you are about six inches away from it—and who wants to look at a picture at a distance of six inches?

A storage cabinet, perhaps one placed under the window, would probably hold more pictures than the average person buys in a lifetime. There's no need to worry about storage space for frames, be-

cause they could perfectly well stay on the walls. With four frames of different sizes and all of your pictures mounted in mats to fit one or another of these four standard frames, you could change your pictures whenever you wanted to, and in about the same way that museums have always done it. Any reliable framer, by the way, can fix the backs so that mats can be slipped in and out conveniently.

The reason for talking about pictures and picture framing at such length is very simple. We are not interested in passing on home decorating advice—useful as such an activity may be. The purpose of this book is to build up an attitude towards the house and all of its parts, an attitude which will help produce a living design adapted in every way to the physical and emotional requirements of the family.

From the attitude stems a course of action. It consists of clearing out everything whose usefulness is doubtful and retaining only those items that stand up under critical examination. This involves analyzing your needs, a provision not ordinarily made.

PLANNING FOR USE

This method of attacking the whole question of how to live can pay the most extraordinary dividends in the most unexpected ways. Take, if you like, the question of the dictionary which most families own. In a surprising number of cases this dictionary is a fairly husky volume. If the library is the living-room, as is usually the case, this dictionary will be tucked away on a bookshelf, and because it is so clumsy to handle, it really doesn't get handled, and the purpose for which it was bought is therefore lost. Nevertheless, there are ways of installing dictionaries in the average home so that their use is made easy, in fact, made definitely attractive. One—and a fairly old one, at that—is the provision of a sloping shelf, somewhere in the

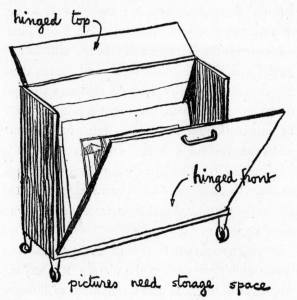

hinged top

hinged front

pictures need storage space

book-shelf section of the room, reserved for the exclusive use of the dictionary. If possible, there should be a small light over it. The normal problems of handling a clumsy book are eliminated by a design which takes care of it. Other solutions would involve the use of one or another of the gadgets sold to libraries and schools, which consist of turning stands built on the principle of a Lazy Susan, or inclined shelves on arms, set into the wall so that they can be swung out of the way.

Is this too much trouble to take for a dictionary? It could be. It depends entirely on how much you want to use one and whether or not you want the children to grow up with the habit of referring to the dictionary when they don't know the meaning of a word.

Design in this sense is an expression, an exceedingly personal expression, of a way of living. Housing the dictionary is part of this way of living, and this problem will be solved or not depending on how you feel about dictionaries. Multiply this process by a thousand, and you have a house that is really designed.

Up to this point we have been looking at the living-room as a series of solutions to very practical problems like the provision of storage space, the proper handling of pictures and special books, flexible seating, getting the right amount of light in the right place, and so on. There are other qualities to be produced which are quite as important in their way but much less tangible.

SPACE

For example, there is the whole question of space, the most vexing problem of all the problems the modern architect has to contend with. Should a living-room look spacious or small? Both kinds are good; a combination is best. Should it be higher than the other rooms or the same? Should it open out to include a porch or a garden, or should it re-

main shut in? Will it have to function at its best with a lot of people in it or just a few? Is it to be formal or informal?

These questions are hard to answer, except in the most specific terms applied to specific problems. Yet answer them we must.

The little sketches below indicate some of the steps to be taken on the way to a solution.

We start with a rectangular box sixteen or eighteen feet wide, twenty or twenty-four feet long, seven and a half to eight and a half feet high. This

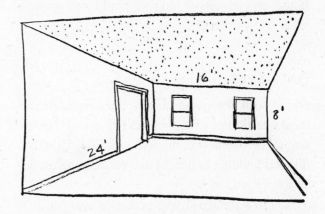

is a good enough size for the better-than-average home. Unfortunately, the better-than-average home rarely gets any further in its design than the provision of this rectangular box.

The nice thing about a box is that it is familiar, easy to design and build. Its disadvantages are that

note balanced daylight

21

it is comparatively inflexible, hard to light, visually uninteresting, and acoustically atrocious.

These sketches, which show one kind of transition from a conventional boxlike interior into one that is better organized for use of indoor and outdoor space, illustrate some of the possibilities at the disposal of the designer today. If the house is largely or entirely a one-story design, the freedom to change ceiling height and the outlines of the room is greater, of course, than if there were a floor above. This is one advantage of the one-story house, and as we go along we shall come across a good many others.

MATERIALS

Along with the question of space comes the related question of what encloses the space. Here we find all the richness of modern technology and traditional building to delight and confuse the would-be home builder.

Not so long ago it was generally assumed that the walls of a room—any room—were finished in plaster, which was either painted or papered, and that was about all. If one could afford it, plaster was replaced by wood paneling in the study and by tiles in the bathroom, and that was really all.

Today the list of materials actually used by architects for the interiors of houses is a very long one. First come the dry sheet materials with which you can make a wall or ceiling in no time at all. Some of these materials are designed to be left exposed. Most of them, however, require painting or papering and are not radically different in appearance from plaster. They are just more convenient to handle. Some of them are insulating boards in addition, which gives them an advantage over plaster.

Then there are the laminated materials—the most common of which is plywood—whose use makes it possible to get a tremendous variety of natural wood finishes without spending much money.

Some architects have used exterior materials inside the house, and with great success. For example, a brick wall is finished as brick inside as well as out. Similarly, you can have walls of natural stone or wood. These devices are used primarily to give the house a unity inside and out that conventional houses seldom have, but in addition they have great decorative effect and the advantage of requiring no maintenance. This is not a new idea; it was used in some of the best of the early Colonial houses.

A rule that the wise home builder should follow is never to use a material that requires maintenance if one can be found that does not. This saves money, to be sure, but far more important, it keeps the house looking well year after year. Houses of permanent materials that do not require maintenance age gracefully and inexpensively. A wall of brick or stone will look as well in a hundred years as it does when built. More accurately, it will look a great deal better, because time deals kindly with such materials, softening their sharp edges and enriching their color.

LIVING ROOMS

One of the nicest things about contemporary design is that it has no set pattern: you can have as much formality or informality as you like, and you can mix these qualities in any way you see fit. Both of the rooms shown on this page, for example, are architecturally severe, but they differ radically in furniture. Room 1 is extremely informal, emphasizing comfort and conviviality. Room 2 shows a carefully studied, even ascetic furniture grouping. The handsome chairs and tables are American-made pieces designed by Alvar Aalto, famous Finnish architect.

3

4

5

Some idea of the variety which modern materials can give the modern interior is shown in these excellent examples of contemporary design and decoration. In all of the rooms, the use of special wall finishes to create a richer background for the furniture is much in evidence: all but one employ decorative plywood paneling, and brick, fieldstone, sand finish plaster, glass block and even wood siding (normally intended for exterior use) have been used in particular cases to add further interest. The transparent glass panels in the upper part of the two-story room, 5, open into a second floor bedroom, joining it with the main living area without sacrificing essential privacy. Views 8 and 9 show a combined living-dining-music room in a recently remodeled house. The sloping ceiling fits under a mono-pitch (shed type) roof. Folding doors open onto a terrace to the south, and clerestory windows in the highest part of the room, facing north, flood the entire space with diffused daylight. The stairway and passage to the second floor bedrooms have been made a prime decorative feature.

6

7

8

9

10

11

Many people believe that if they are to have a modern house they must throw away all of their traditional furniture. This is simply not so. As these traditionally-furnished modern rooms demonstrate, the smooth, unadorned surfaces characteristic of contemporary design afford an excellent background for ornate period pieces. Modern and traditional architecture can even be combined in the same room, as in view 10, which shows the living room of a modernized Pennsylvania farmhouse in which all of the new construction was carried out in the modern style. Room 12 shows a dramatic use of glass block in the upper part of a two-story window-wall.

13

14

Not all modern interiors are bare, nor need they be unless you happen to like bare rooms. Good contemporary design varies all the way from the severe simplicity of the apartment living room shown in view 13 to the rich warmth of room 17 or even combines the two effects, as has been done in the combination study-living room pictured in 15. View 16 shows the living room in a city house, designed especially for entertainment and carefully studied to produce ideal acoustical conditions. The glass wall looks out on an enclosed, and therefore completely private, court around which the house was built.

16

17

18

19

20

Pattern and decoration may be provided by the furnishings, by construction materials, or even by certain essential equipment—as in the case of the
corrugated ceiling panels which furnish radiant heat
for the story-and-a-half living room shown in picture
21. Sometimes the most important decorative
element may be the view outside the window, as
in room 22. In the city apartment shown in 18, a
glass block wall serves the dual purpose of shutting
out street noises and providing light and an interesting background for the furnishings; the simplicity
of room 20 is set off by a ceiling of v-jointed boards.
And, as picture 19 shows, a rough stone fireplace
can be just as much at home in a modern interior
as in its traditional setting.

23

24

25

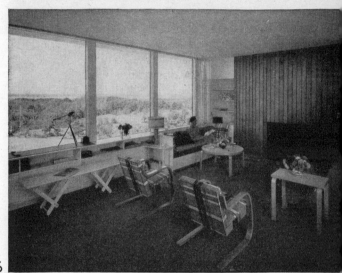

26

27

Some of the drama which large glass areas make possible is suggested by picture 23, which shows the living room of a beach house overlooking the ocean (picture 24 shows the opposite side of the same room). That similar effects can be achieved on a smaller scale is demonstrated by the other rooms shown, all of which employ walls of fixed and movable glass to add to the feeling of space.

28

29

30

The large window—modern architecture's most important contribution to house design—can be used in a great variety of ways. In 28, the designer has employed a series of large, fixed lights separated by structural posts to form the entire view side of a second-floor living room. In 29, the living room has been divided into two parts by use of fixed, floor-to-ceiling glass —flanked by ventilating sash—in one portion of the space. Views 31 and 32 show a large, two-level living room which combines a glass wall opening onto a terrace with a projecting plant window at one end. Picture 30 shows still another window treatment employing a checkerboard of wood mullions to support fixed glass. Big glass areas of this type have been used as successfully in the northern part of the country as in the south and in California.

33

34

35

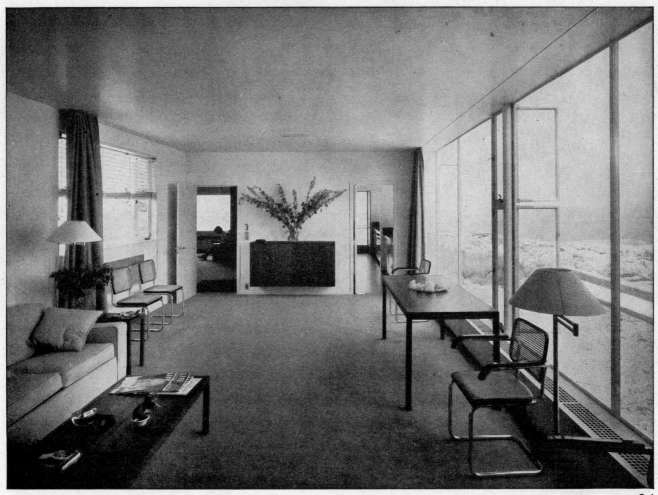

36

37

Planned furniture arrangement, worked out for convenience as well as appearance, is another important contribution of modern architecture. Pictures 33 and 34 show two views of a large living room designed with a definite use-pattern in mind. In this example, notice how two entirely different furniture groups have been provided—one around the fireplace, the other, mostly for daytime use, near the large windows. In 35, a terrace window takes the place of the conventional fireplace as the focus for the main furniture group. Pictures 36 and 37 show how similar planning principles are applied to less pretentious houses.

CHAPTER FOUR

WHERE SHALL WE EAT?

THOSE OF US who grew up in the traditional middle-class home of thirty or forty years ago remember quite clearly that dining was never much of a problem. There was a large kitchen with a table in it for the hired girl—newly arrived, in all probability, from Sweden, Ireland, or Poland. She was an affable, immensely competent person who could whip up anything from a snack to a banquet at short notice and somehow managed to do not only the cooking and dishwashing but the serving as well. For dining, the family had the dining-room. Everyone who was anybody had a dining-room. The notion of eating anywhere else would have been considered very strange indeed.

Because families were bigger, the dining-room was a pretty ample space, and its already large table in the center could be expanded with leaves so that a dozen people could sit down together for Thanksgiving or Christmas dinner. Over the center of the table, hanging on gilt brass chains, was the most ornate lighting fixture in the house. It usually had at least three lamps and a dazzling array of stained glass. This fixture was not only the fanciest piece of applied art in the house of the period, it was also the most efficient. And presently, in discussing the dining-room of today, we shall find that we come back to it.

In the early 1900's a tablecloth with folding pads underneath was considered a "must." Few, if any, people had even dreamed of replacing the expensive, hard-to-launder tablecloth with today's place mats. As a result there was a second piece of furniture in the room—a sideboard, which was really a linen closet turned on its side and set up on legs. This contained the tablecloths for everyday dining and formal family dinners, and the wonderful lace contraptions which were spread out only on the most impressive of ceremonial occasions. The top of the sideboard contained the silver, which, if Father had made any money at all, was almost as hard to lift as it was to clean. This alone kept the maid pretty busy, for gleaming silver was the hallmark of a properly run household. But this was not all. Somewhere else in the room there was a great glass-and-wood cage, usually with an intricately carved front behind which the family kept its real treasures. There was the set of china that Grandmother had brought back from her wedding trip to Germany. There were the porcelain shepherds and shepherdesses made perhaps in the kilns of Carlsbad or in one of the great establishments outside Paris. There were little china dogs and cats from the famous English works. And perhaps a polished piece of stone presented to the family by Uncle Ezra on his return from a trip to the Petrified Forest. There were cut glass pitchers so ornate

The dining room was a family social center

that Mother really hated to pour water out of them. There were small bottles filled with sand from the beach at Nassau or Bermuda, surrounded, no doubt, by the inevitable collection of seashells.

All these treasures needed space, and they got space. Nothing could be farther from our minds today than a desire to ridicule them. The old-style dining-room was a fine thing—and let's not forget it. It was a family social center. It was so comfortable that people sat for long hours after dinner, swapping stories, cracking nuts, and drinking wine. Because it had the only decent lighting fixture in the whole house, this was where the children did their homework, and where games were played. Special tables for whist were to be found only in a few big houses, and the folding card table was not yet what it has since become.

This picture lasted into the twenties, when two things happened simultaneously. First was the surge of prosperity which swept the country from one end to the other and reached its peak in 1929. Second was the fact that Greta the maid had found that she could make more money and live much more pleasantly if she got a job in a store or office.

Because of these two things, something new appeared in the middle-class house. The dining-room remained, but a brand-new element, the breakfast nook, was added. This was sometimes part of the pantry, sometimes a separate little sunroom with benches for four and a table in between. The breakfast nook was both a sign of the general inflation going on at the time and a very practical response to the shortage of servants. The family began to do most of its eating in the breakfast room, because it meant less work and fewer steps for Mother, who was now the cook. The dining-room turned into a kind of architectural vermiform appendix, which was kept because the operation of removing it had not yet become fashionable.

The next stage occurred in the thirties, when, as Macy's puts it, it became smart to be thrifty. Suddenly a split arose in the ranks of the house planners. By now money was scarce, and something had to be done to provide adequate houses within shrinking budgets. The dining-room was the logical victim. Elaborate scientific studies were made to prove that here was a room which should never have existed in the first place—it took up many cubic feet of space in the house but was used only three or four hours out of the twenty-four. This, they cried, was inefficient—and the era of the living-dining-room was inaugurated.

The more modern-minded architects saw a number of rather interesting features in the living-dining-room. They were being forced to make living-rooms smaller—again because of shrinking income—and they didn't like it. Moreover, some space had also to be provided for eating. By using one end of the room for this purpose, or perhaps an alcove, they were able to create the illusion of more space than actually existed for general living purposes. But once the first flush of enthusiasm for the new idea began to wear off, it became obvious that here was no millennium. The living-dining-room was a makeshift, frequently quite satisfactory, to be sure, but nevertheless an expedient to save space and money. For family meals it worked fairly well, although the peace of the living-room in the evening was sometimes shattered by the setting of the table at the beginning of the meal and the removal of the dishes at the end. Moreover, the kitchen was now next to the living-room, and the clatter of dishes being washed came through the swinging door so clearly that people began to wonder why they bothered to have a door. For formal meals, dining in the living-room was much less satisfactory, because while the family might have hardened itself to these new inconveniences, there was no reason to inflict them on the guests.

This brings us to today. As far as the middle-income family is concerned, the maid-of-all-work is farther away than ever. Budgets are more ample than they were during the depression years, but more and more money is being diverted from space into equipment, most of which is by no means gadgetry of a luxury nature but machinery which must be purchased to make up for the lack of available labor.

So the problem of the forties is much the same as it was in the thirties. The temper of the people, however, is not the same. There is evidence of a growing desire to recreate certain aspects of social life within the home on something approximating the old-time basis. Its reflection in the work of modern-minded architects is very interesting. Among these architects, who are still comparatively few in number, there is this feeling about dining: that no arrangement is acceptable unless a definite space can be established where meals may be set up and cleared away without causing disturbance to any other part of the house.

AN ANALYSIS OF DINING

There are five places where a family can have its meals: it can eat (1) in the dining-room; (2) in the living-room; (3) in the kitchen; (4) in a breakfast nook; and (5) outside. It is perfectly clear from these possibilities that the dining-room is ideal if service facilities exist; that the living-room is only partly satisfactory; that the same is true for the kitchen (at least, the kitchen the way it is today); that the breakfast nook to do a complete job must really become another version of the dining-room; and that meals outside are either a seasonal affair or confined to limited sections of the country.

There is another way of analyzing eating requirements. We have (1) family meals; (2) meals for the younger children, probably served separately; (3) formal dinners with or without guests; and (4) snacks—whether at midnight or any other time.

How these requirements are met is a decision primarily for the family rather than the architect. If you won't consider giving a formal dinner anywhere but in a separate dining-room and the budget won't stand the cost, formal dinners will have to go by the boards. Should family meals in the kitchen seem most practical except for a prejudice against dining in a cold, white room, consider the possibility of treating the kitchen as the warmest, most cheerful room in the house.

41

Solving the problem of where to eat, however, is not nearly as uncompromising a matter as it used to be. There are all sorts of new solutions: some are so unconventional that the kinds of space developed do not yet have generally accepted names.

THE ROOM THAT WAS NEVER LIVED IN

One of the first proposals of this kind was a room in an exhibit at the New York World's Fair. It was designed by Allmon Fordyce.

Fordyce's approach to the problem was based on an analysis similar to the one just outlined, and he decided that a solution worth trying was an entirely new kind of room, which he called the kitchen-living room. In this room there were easy chairs and a dining space and all of the cooking and dishwashing facilities. It was divided by a kitchen counter which contained a sink, with cupboards and shelves above. Instead of a white stove and refrigerator, these fixtures were a dull midnight blue. The white sink was replaced by gleaming metal, and everything else in the room, including the cupboards, was carried out in natural color wood. If the "ooh's" and "ah's" in front of this exhibit could have been converted into shiny five-cent pieces, architect Fordyce would have been a very wealthy man by the time the Fair closed, because people saw in this design not just a good-looking kitchen, but a brand-new way to live in a house. Here was a kitchen which accepted the fact that nobody except the very rich was going to have servants. The kitchen-living room not only lightened the burden of housework, but it was also good-looking enough for guests. This was a completely new idea and yet a very old one: Fordyce had simply resurrected and modernized the old farmhouse kitchen.

During the next few years other versions of the kitchen-living room appeared in various parts of the country. Generally, the reaction was pretty favorable. Somehow this new kind of space corresponded not only to an economic situation but also to a changing idea of how to live. The snobbery of the twenties disappeared. No one thought it strange that the housewife should do the cooking and that guests should help with the dishes.

Meanwhile, designers were finding that there were almost as many variations to the living-kitchen idea as there were families. In 1943 magazines showed a kitchen designed for the Libbey-Owens-Ford Glass Company. Use of a sliding wall made it possible not only to open the kitchen to the dining and recreation area, but even to merge these spaces with the living-room on occasion. A series of hardwood covers for sink, stove, and other equipment converted the work area into an interior handsome enough to glamorize any buffet supper. This ingenious publicity device was nothing more than a re-use of many separate ideas which had been suggested by many different architects. It proved that one could have a living kitchen or a more conventional arrangement, depending on the position the sliding wall happened to occupy.

We like the living kitchen. We think it solves many problems which would otherwise stump the family of moderate means. But maybe you don't like it at all. What then? Who is right? The thing about houses that makes designing them so endlessly fascinating is that everyone can be right. If your life is not complete without a room devoted solely to dining, if the idea of eating in the same room where food is prepared is revolting, it is your inalienable right to demand a dining-room. There is nothing whatever wrong with that. Just remember that it costs more than no dining-room, which brings us back to where we started—to tastes and budgets.

NEW PROBLEMS

While we now seem to have a solution which can be worked out with a great number of variations, we also have new problems. One is the matter of acoustics, and you will find considerable discussion of sound control in the kitchen in another chapter. This much, however, is worth emphasizing here: The more flexible a plan becomes, and the more it relies on open spaces which can be subdivided or merged at will, the more acute becomes the problem of acoustics. The kitchen is a natural noise-producing center, and what sounds cannot be stopped at their source must be absorbed in one way or another by the ceiling and walls and floor.

There is also the problem of cooking odors, which are now free to move through the entire living area of the house. This is discussed in Chapter X.

Lighting also becomes a problem, because one kind is needed for the work center, another for the dining table, and a third for the living area. If spaces are to be related in a flexible manner and activities overlap, lighting will also have to be flexible. Equipment to meet all these problems exists.

VARYING THE ROUTINE

One of the most wonderful houses ever built is Taliesen, the home of Frank Lloyd Wright, out in the hills of Wisconsin. It is an immense, rambling sort of structure, which today is beyond the means of any except the most wealthy. One thing that strikes the visitor most forcibly about this house is not so much its size or cost, but the manner in which the architect and his family and students vary the eating routine; with little difficulty and considerable satisfaction. In addition to the separate dining-room where everyone generally eats, there are little terraces here and there where on good days meals can be taken on wheeled serving tables. And there are also built-in tables in the living-room and sitting-room.

The same possibilities should be considered for a house on a much smaller scale—even the average-size house built for four or five people and containing three or possibly four bedrooms. If there is a fireplace in the master bedroom, there is no reason at all why this space should not be used on occasion—not by the whole family, of course, but by one or both of the parents. Small outdoor sitting spaces, whether sheltered or open to the sky, are equally usable if planned in convenient relation to the kitchen. The living-room or the library alcove could have similar provisions.

This part of dining has nothing whatever to do with efficiency, but with the fact that family life, due to the necessary repetition of a number of uninteresting chores, can become extremely dull, and even slight variations from normal habits can provide a considerable lift.

This seemingly minor problem was left to the end because it highlights what should be the fundamental approach to planning. Questions of efficiency, mechanical design, lighting, acoustics, and so on, are important; but they should be solved and brushed out of the way as fast as possible. The basic requirement is to provide a framework for living, not for running machinery—and this is the foundation on which really successful planning must ultimately be carried out. The broader the picture of how to live, the better the plan. If this extends to an occasional snack in front of the fireplace, so much the better. It is the joint responsibility of the family and the architect to see to it that not a single one of these small enrichments to the pattern of daily existence is omitted.

CHAPTER FIVE

LIGHTING

FOR MANY YEARS lighting in the home has been provided as an afterthought. It was conceived in terms of fixtures rather than illumination and occupied an almost negligible place in the building budget. For this reason the interior of the average home, which should be the best-lighted interior that could be designed, is among the worst. People do their evening chores, homework, bridge playing, reading—in fact, carry on practically all home activities—under lighting conditions which the owner of the corner delicatessen would not tolerate for a moment and which would run a factory owner out of business in no time.

Homes are badly lighted, but not because of lack of knowledge. Quite the contrary is true. Our technicians know a great deal about lighting, and the purpose of this chapter is to describe some of the things they have found out. Since lighting experts are not hired, as a rule, to work on designs for the home, many of our examples will be commercial or industrial. The fundamental principles of good illumination, however, are the same. If we seem to wander away from the house from time to time, these digressions will not be irrelevant.

We are going to start to talk about lighting in terms of the eye rather than the fixtures. Illumination is something related to seeing, and only to seeing. Consequently nothing could be more to the point in a discussion of lighting than an understanding of the peculiar limitations of the eye and

its extraordinary latitude. A number of technical terms are going to be used, but not one represents an idea that is too complicated to grasp, and each has to be understood before home illumination can be discussed with any degree of sense.

THE PROBLEM OF THE TUNNEL

When the Holland Tunnel was built, the engineers who designed it were very conscious of the importance of this great project for linking Manhattan with New Jersey, and they tried to make their calculations as nearly perfect as possible. This was particularly true of the lighting, for with the immense volume of automobile traffic planned, no single factor was more vital in assuring a safe and steady flow of cars. After the tunnel was completed, it was discovered that the lighting, for all the trouble taken with it, was anything but perfect. It was also found that there was no such thing as an "ideal" amount of light.

This is what was the trouble. Drivers who entered the tunnel on a brilliantly clear day invariably found the inside quite dark at first. This was caused by the difference in intensity between full sunlight and the lamp light in the tunnel, and there is not as yet any practical apparatus for lighting things as brightly as the sun does. Moreover, on entering the tunnel after dusk, the same group of drivers found the same intensity of illumination too great. In other words, "perfect" lighting for the Holland Tunnel was not a fixed quantity at all. To work properly at all times it would have to vary in intensity, depending on what was going on outside. The same problem, in a different form, appears in the home.

THE PROBLEM OF THE NIGHT BOMBERS

Some years ago, when the RAF began its great bombing raids over Germany, there were many stories of how the fliers were conditioned for their hazardous night missions. They were fed carrots. They were kept in darkened rooms for hours, so that retinal sensitivity would be increased to a maximum. Everything which could be imagined was done to reduce the pilots' difficulties in distinguishing the targets they were to find and destroy. For a while everything went well.

One night a fleet of Lancasters and Halifaxes, probing its way to the heart of Germany, approached one of the industrial cities. It was greeted, not by the customary blackout, but by a barrage of intense light thrown up by hundreds of searchlights. The result was the same as being awakened in the middle of the night by a flashlight in one's face—complete inability to see anything. New procedures had to be developed to meet this new weapon.

We have here two very clear illustrations of the inability of the eye to adjust itself rapidly to extremes of intensity. The British fliers, for instance, would not have been particularly disturbed by the searchlight barrage had they not been conditioned to be almost abnormally sensitive to light. Had they flown over in brightly lighted planes the story would have been quite different. The drivers in the Holland Tunnel had the same difficulty in adjusting themselves to comparative extremes of intensity within a split second.

Because improper lighting in a vehicular tunnel could mean terrible accidents with disruption of traffic as well as loss of life, engineers—the very best that could be found—were engaged to work on this problem. Because the British high command could not afford to waste a single night raider, they, too, gave their lighting problem the most expert attention obtainable. But improper lighting in the home doesn't kill anybody or cost measurable amounts of money or produce any other immediately noticeable effect, and in consequence it has been pretty largely ignored. To be sure, it is a far cry from the RAF to the reading corner in the living-room. But it isn't as far as it seems.

HOW MUCH LIGHT IS ENOUGH?

The question of enough light is something most people think about, though not necessarily in very precise terms. Did you ever go down to the local electrical supply store and wonder what wattage bulb to get for a certain fixture? One reason it is hard to choose is that the quantity of illumination by which the eye can function varies almost beyond belief. If the light by which you are reading this book comes from a floor or table lamp, the illumination on the page is probably somewhere between five and fifteen foot-candles. (A foot-candle is the quantity of light thrown by a single candle on some point a foot away from the flame.) If tomorrow afternoon you were to take the book outdoors and read in the shade of a tree, however, the illumination would be around 500 foot-candles, or thirty to one hundred times as much. And, as far as comfort is concerned, it would be hard to tell the difference.

"Fine!" one might say at this point. "This little fact will save me a lot. If one can read at almost any intensity, why waste good money on unneeded wattage?" The eye is a willing and wonderfully adaptable instrument; if necessary it will function admirably for reading even by firelight. Unfortunately, while we can see remarkably well under extremely unfavorable conditions, there is a muscular and nervous strain involved and a disproportionate amount of energy expended. So this saving would not pay off nearly as well as one might think. In the first place, as the intensity is lowered, we see more *slowly*. This has been proved by an experiment repeated so many times in hundreds of factories that industrialists now take it for granted. People have been given jobs to do with *X* foot-candles of illumination on their work; then the intensity was stepped up, for the same work. It was found every time that as brightness increases, the rate at which the work is accomplished increases with it. Up to a certain point the amount of work done increases in direct proportion to the amount of illumination. After this point is passed—it is in the neighborhood of 100 foot-candles—the quantity of work continues to increase, but no longer at the same rate as the illumination. Finally the amount of work increase levels off almost entirely.

It might be thought that somewhere around 100 foot-candles would be the most efficient level of illumination. But continuing the experiment produced another fact: above the point where the rate of work failed to increase, fatigue continued to decrease sharply. The experiment demonstrated two things very clearly: with more light we not only see more *quickly*, but more *easily* as well. In this latter respect there seems to be almost no limit to the amount of light we can profitably use. It might be noted that even 100 foot-candles is way beyond the level of illumination we are accustomed to in homes and offices.

In the best of the modern factories, fluorescent or mercury-vapor lamps are jammed together so tightly above the tools and assembly lines that some interiors seem to have a solid ceiling of light. At the Dodge Chicago plant, largest producer of airplane engines, no less than $2,700,000 was spent on the lighting installation alone. And every penny of this sizable investment was made by men who do not buy things for factories unless they pay off in terms of production. Matthew Luckiesh—probably the outstanding authority on lighting—seems to consider the best factory installations not yet good enough, for his investigations have led him to recommend intensities at working levels of 500 to 1,000 foot-candles for some operations, running as high as 3,000 for tailors who work on blue serge. A few years ago such levels of brightness would have been considered unthinkable.

The first facts to be noted about intensity, therefore, are (1) that our eyes are extremely bad judges of quantity of illumination; and (2) that so far as productivity, comfort, and health are concerned, we can scarcely get enough light. Point one can be taken care of by using the services offered by most local offices of the electric light companies, which will provide data on desirable levels of illuminations, lamps necessary, etc. Some will even send around a man with a light meter to check the present installation. Point two is partly a matter of budget, since current costs money, and partly a matter of fixture design. Lamps with tight, heavy shades can absorb most of the light paid for before it gets into the room.

"Enough light" is not the whole story. We have all experienced the unpleasant sensation of suddenly entering a room that was "too brightly lighted." The same effect is sometimes produced by a show window on a dark street. The *quantity* of illumination is not the important thing here, but the *sudden change* in quantity. The show window, for instance, might have been lighted to 150 foot-candles, the room to 100—and yet a pleasant view from a mountain may be lighted to as much as 5,000 foot-candles by the summer sun. The catch is that what we consider too much or too little in the way of light is a matter of where we have been

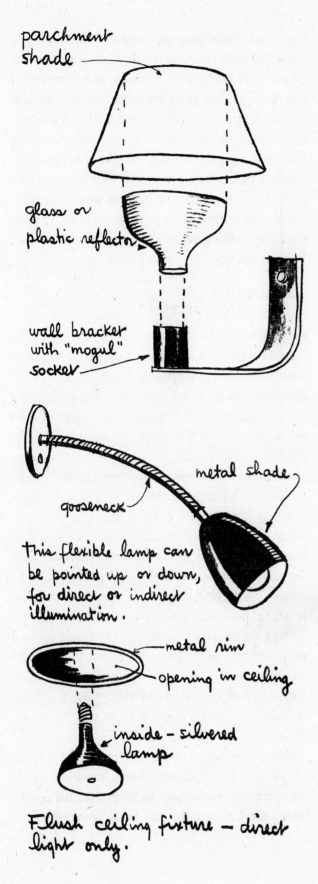

parchment shade

glass or plastic reflector

wall bracket with "mogul" socket

gooseneck

metal shade

This flexible lamp can be pointed up or down, for direct or indirect illumination.

metal rim

opening in ceiling

inside-silvered lamp

Flush ceiling fixture — direct light only.

just before entering or looking into the space in question.

A while back it was stated that from the problems of the RAF to those of lighting a corner of the living-room was not a very far cry. It is equally true for the shop window and the factory. In all cases the eye is at the receiving end, and some apparatus at the other. Eyes have to function in safety and comfort whether at a turret lathe or the evening paper. There are many industrial jobs far less exacting than darning socks, as far as seeing is concerned. It is as important to have sufficient light for home tasks as for operations on the production line, even if the home tasks never appear on any balance sheet. But "enough light" doesn't do the job if the lighting is all out of proportion to the general illumination of the room. And the general illumination, in turn, must be so scaled that it is not blinding to eyes that have been "dark adapted" —like those of the British night fliers—by a walk home through poorly lighted streets.

It appears, therefore, that while intensity is a vital consideration in proper lighting design, it is by no means the only one. Contrast is the next factor to be considered. Just what does this mean?

CONTRAST

Let us imagine that a person is sitting in his favorite armchair, reading a magazine by the light of a floor lamp that has a 100-watt bulb. This lamp, shining on the magazine's page at a distance of three feet, produces the relatively low intensity of twenty foot-candles. But there is no other light in the room, so that areas around the magazine are only dimly illuminated by the stray light from the lamp. The foot-candle intensity of these areas will be one foot-candle at most, producing a contrast ratio of twenty to one between the white page and the surrounding areas. Thus if the person reading

47

has occasion to look away from the page from time to time, his eyes have to adjust themselves very rapidly to a considerable change in brightness. This is hard work, and the demands made on the eye are serious. When the eye first turns from brightness to darkness, the iris has to open up to its widest aperture, quantities of retinal fluid have to be generated very quickly; and even with these great efforts on the part of the eye, it takes a few seconds before anything can be distinguished in the comparative obscurity. Then, when the eye turns back to the bright page, the reverse process has to be gone through, with the result that for a moment you have an uncomfortable feeling that the page is much too bright and glaring.

Now consider another case of contrast. Imagine a living-room in which there is a central lighting fixture containing a single exposed bulb—say, 1,000 watts. The room would be very brightly lighted, but it would also be very badly illuminated, in spite of the amount of money being spent to run the 1,000-watt lamp. It would be bad because the light source would be visible from all parts of the room and would therefore be a source of discomfort; because every shadow cast would be relatively black; and because *the very brightness of the illumination would defeat the purpose of seeing.* One can see into a shadow only when some light issues into it, either by reflection or directly. The

glare and shadows

sun, incidentally, gives the same kind of lighting as the 1,000-watt lamp: it is a brilliant point source which casts sharp, dark shadows. It is the custom to talk of the sun as an ideal kind of illumination. It is, if you perform the simplest, most "natural" activities in sunlight. But it is very bad indeed for the many complicated jobs eyes have to do under modern conditions. Therefore, while the sun will appear again in this discussion, it must be understood that proper room lighting is far more complex than setting up a single bright source of illumination.

BUILDING UP
A LIGHTING PATTERN

One place to look for more clues to good home lighting is in the newer retail shops. Here the same trend appears that was noted in the factories: ever-increasing intensity of light. We also find special characteristics which stem from the nature of a retail business, but these can be disregarded. The modern shop has a high level of over-all illumination. This may be provided by strips of fluorescent lamps or cold cathode tubing, by coves, by high-intensity incandescent fixtures, and by a variety of other equipment. Over and above this general illumination there is special lighting. There are light fixtures for showcases and built-in displays, spotlights for particular items of merchandise, and lenses set flush with the ceiling to provide powerful down light at certain locations. These add up to a lot of ways to illuminate a shop, but the progressive merchant of today, like the progressive industrialist, is finding that he can hardly have too many of these fixtures for the job he would like to see done.

Did it ever occur to you to consider how much simpler it is to light a store than a home? After all, the merchant has merely to illuminate his goods, which are for the most part in the same places all

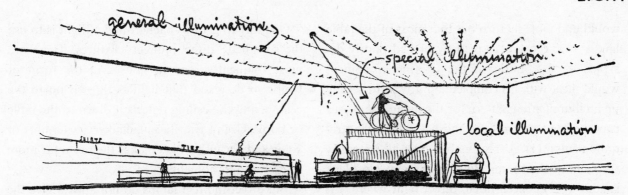

the time, get enough light in the store as a whole so that people can see their way around comfortably, and attract attention to a few special items by means of spotlights. Compare this with the problems of the home, where the light for eating must be variable in intensity and directed down to the table; the light for reading (which may be done after dinner at the table) must be brilliant, and the surrounding areas must be bright. Conversation in the living-room needs a dim arrangement, a few soft pools of light serving more for decoration than illumination. For constant sewing we have already noted Mr. Luckiesh's recommendation of 3,000 foot-candles, a standard which could be met only by use of very special equipment. For reading in the bedroom one kind of illumination is needed, and for dressing in the same room a totally different type is needed. There should be night lights in the bedrooms bright enough to see by, but arranged in such a way that the children won't be awakened. And so on.

The job of lighting the small house is just as exacting as the job of lighting the local department store. Yet the normal investment is less than a hundred dollars for the wiring, and a few dollars more are thrown in for the necessary wall and ceiling fixtures. When next you hear someone predicting a better, cheaper home of the future, think for a moment of what it would cost to produce anything approximating adequate illumination.

Expenditures for lighting have to be increased because they have never been up to normal. Even the houses of the very rich suffer in this respect, not because of lack of funds, but because there was no understanding on the part of the owner or architect of what should be done. Today the story is different. There is a vast accumulated experience which cost hundreds of thousands of dollars to acquire but is now at your architect's disposal for practically nothing.

ENTER THE EXPERT

Let's assume that you are building a new home, remodeling the old one, or fixing up an apartment, and you have called in a lighting consultant. A trip through the rooms might prove instructive. A specialist worthy of the name will not talk fixtures primarily; this much should be clear from what has already been written. He will talk about certain qualities to be created through the use of specific equipment. He will be interested in getting results.

If our expert started on the living-room, he would probably point out a number of deficiencies right away. If there are any of those silly little wall brackets builders inserted so freely into dwellings a few years back, he would undoubtedly suggest tearing them out. They are annoying to look at, clutter up the wall, catch dust, and don't give any light worth mentioning. He might criticize the floor lamps as being clumsy, space-wasting fixtures. It would undoubtedly turn out that most of the table lamps were too low to read by or had poorly designed shades. Little of the lighting equipment would meet with his complete approval. In setting up an illumination pattern for the living-room, our expert would probably establish the following requirements: (1) A reasonable over-all intensity throughout the room. No dim corners. No black shadows; (2) concentrated, direct light where it is needed; (2) flexibility, both in placing of light and in intensity.

Meeting these requirements is highly technical, and not easy, but the ideas are simple. Point (1), for example, means that the room must be flooded with light, and the common procedure is to install some kind of fixture that throws light up to a white ceiling which, in turn, reflects the light back to all parts of the room. This can be done with a lighting cove that goes all around the edges of the ceiling, or with lamps that direct light up instead of down. The ceiling itself might be luminous, that is, made of glass or plastic with lights behind. For a home such a procedure at the moment is far too costly and quite unnecessary.

In a room filled with indirect light the illumination is good in the sense that there are no deep shadows, and light is diffused throughout the area. But it is not pleasant illumination. There is no contrast. Objects seem to lose their sharpness and solidity. Indirect lighting is "flat." Therefore, in the well-designed living-room it provides only the background, not the main illumination.

pools of light are decorative

One way to get this background of light is to use the so-called "direct-indirect" fixtures. These are most frequently seen in houses in the form of lamps so designed that light is thrown up to the ceiling, and the ceiling reflects it down to the table or book. Use of translucent shades gives a note of color and warmth which makes the room far more attractive and homelike.

But direct-indirect lamps do not always give the needed amount of light for reading, writing, or sewing. This is where point (2) comes in. Concentrated light can be provided in a great variety of ways. A bulb in a reflector will do it. So will any of the inside-silvered lamps which are seen so often in show windows and art galleries. There are lens-type spotlights which can be built directly into the ceiling so that only a flush piece of glass shows. Also available are the small spotlights used for display purposes in stores. Some of these will seem inappropriate for use in the living-room. If the idea of a spotlight fastened to the wall strikes you as too radical, use a more conventional solution such as table lamps with properly designed shades. The point is: concentrated, direct light must be provided where it is needed.

At this stage in the process the room may be said to be well lighted and agreeable in appearance. There is a general glow of light everywhere, probably provided by indirect lighting. There are pools of light created by individual lamps. And if one wants to read or sew, a strong light source is available. But there still remains one problem to be solved.

If people always did their reading in exactly the same place; if they always sat in the same grouping; if they always carried on the same activities— *if* these things were true, a fixed lighting scheme would be the answer. But they are not true. Sometimes people talk but do not read. For this less light is required. Sometimes they listen to the radio and don't talk. This requires still less light. These and

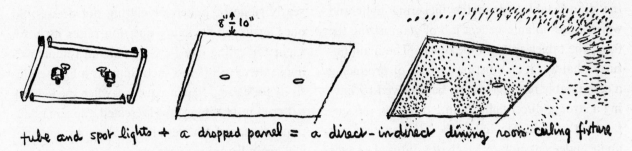

tube and spot lights + a dropped panel = a direct-indirect dining room ceiling fixture

other shifts in the use of the room demand lighting that is not only adequate and attractive, but flexible as well.

On the stage, if less illumination is required, the electrician merely operates his dimmers until the desired level is reached. Few homes today can afford such controls. But they can afford the extra switches and wiring that will do approximately the same job. In other words, the living-room should be so equipped that the wall switches control two or three lighting patterns. Another control possibility is afforded by the three-way lamp, which is being used more and more in floor and table lamps. There are also fixtures which tilt up or down to become direct or indirect. Electrical supply stores have sockets so built that the bulb can be pointed in almost any direction. These devices are excellent for the direct-type lighting units mentioned above. Gadgets such as swivel sockets and extra switches are not recommended for their own sake: they add flexibility and control to the conventional lighting pattern.

"More light" is a slogan that could be applied with profit to almost any room in any house. When considering the living-room, don't be afraid of making it too bright. The intimacy of an attractive room comes not from dimness, but from the *balance* of the different kinds of illumination. This, by the way, is easy to prove. If the bulbs in your present lamps were taken out and replaced by photofloods, which have perhaps fifteen times the light output, the room would be much brighter, but the character of the lighting would not be changed

greatly. Should you want to try this experiment, photofloods can be purchased at any photographic supply store. But don't leave them in the lamps! Photofloods have a rated life of only two to six hours.

LIGHT FOR EATING

We need light to eat by as well as for reading. But illumination of the dining-room is a vastly different problem from illumination of the living-room. The dining table, normally, is a fixed object. The people who use it are, for the period of the meal, equally fixed in their positions. This means that the lighting scheme can be more static.

The only light needed for eating is light on the table. Background illumination has only to be sufficiently bright to reduce excessive contrast between the table and its surroundings. But light for the table is not merely illumination: let us remember that the one place in the modern home where the candle still has any functional justification is on

any table + good lighting = secondary desk

the dinner table, where the flickering light and warm color do an excellent job of glamorizing the food, the tableware, and the diners. The main fixture, whatever it is, must be capable of producing a comparable result. This can be achieved by having a strong, direct light shining down on the surface of the table. The light is best if it comes from an incandescent bulb rather than a diffused surface such as a fluorescent tube. The closer the light resembles a "point source"—that is, the bare filament of the lamp—the more pronounced the glitter will be, and the glitter of dishes, glassware, and silver is one of the things that makes a dining-room table good to look at. Direct downward lighting has another function: striking the surface of the table, it bounces back up and provides a certain amount of illumination for the room as a whole. The best design, however, does not rely entirely on this reflected light, but provides a secondary light source which gives general illumination for the room.

Types and sizes of fixtures for the dining-room are legion. One safe rule in their selection is that the simpler and less conspicuous they are, the better. One example of the rule carried to an extreme is the concealed spotlight that shines down through a small hole in the ceiling. Here the source has been made practically invisible, and results are sometimes dramatic. Variations include bulbs on the ceiling, so shielded with metal baffles that the source of the light is very inconspicuous. Concealed lamps, while theatrical in their effectiveness, have a disadvantage. It is not that they can't do a good job, but that dining tables are rarely used only for eating.

Light for dining, in the average home, is almost always used for other pursuits in addition to eating. For one thing, some dining takes place in the kitchen and in the living-room. Many houses have no dining-rooms at all. And if they do, the table is probably taken over for homework, for the semi-

yearly game of poker, or cutting out dresses. So once again the flexibility question raises its head. Light for eating can be fixed. But in tomorrow's house there will be no such thing as a light exclusively for eating. In consequence, when the lighting pattern for the dining area is created, the same solutions discussed for certain living-room activities will again be appropriate.

LIGHTING FOR SPECIAL FUNCTIONS

By now the ways of our hypothetical expert should be more clear. He is concerned with illumination, not with chandeliers and imitation candles. In each room he seizes upon the major and minor activities and tailors the lighting to fit. His approach is creative, not conventional. It is the same as the approach of the modern architect to planning. Nowhere does this attitude express itself more clearly than in the solutions for special lighting functions.

In a child's bedroom, for example, the expert would borrow the idea of enclosed lights, set flush with the baseboard, from standard hospital practice. Such lights would be rather nice in halls, too, and they aren't impossibly expensive.

We have become accustomed to lights in refrigerators and clothes closets. In the new bureaus that are being treated as built-ins rather than loose pieces of furniture, why not lights in the drawers?

built-in keyhole lights should be standard equipment.

Anyone who ever tried to find a pair of dark socks on a dim winter's morning would bless the manufacturer for the rest of his days. At the moment bureau lights sound expensive, but even the cheapest cars have lights in their glove compartments.

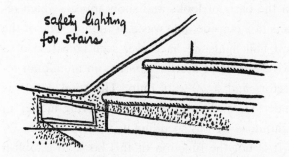

safety lighting for stairs

Most of us take for granted the existence of a fairly good lighting set-up for the bathroom mirror. But there are other mirrors in the house where people apply lipstick, straighten hats, and so on, where equally good illumination is needed. There is no particular trick in making mirrors that have their own little lighting systems built in.

Recent models of cars are almost sure to have a tiny light in the dashboard which illuminates the area where the ignition key goes in. Yet there is nowhere that one can buy a similarly convenient gadget for the front or rear door keyhole. For an ingenious architect, providing such a convenience would be no problem at all.

Theaters with stairs have small lights built into the top and bottom steps of each flight—a wise and economical safety measure. Did you ever see a house so equipped? Yet insurance companies are always releasing horrifying statistics on the number of accidents that take place on stairs in the home. Theaters have another device which is agreeable and inexpensive: tube lights (the same as those in neon signs) in hollow railings along the aisles. A stair illuminated in this manner would be safe, and unusually good looking as well.

One of us once visited a house in the Middle West which had a very remarkable lighting unit in the dining-room. It was an elaborate gadget of frosted glass, containing three lamps—red, blue, and yellow—each controlled by its own switch and dimmer. The controls were located in the pantry. The system, of course, was borrowed from theater footlights. By fooling around with three knobs on the pantry wall, the owner was able to get almost any color and intensity of light he wanted. All three lights turned on full, for instance, produced white. The red and blue produced various shades of violet; the yellow and blue, various shades of green; and all three used together but in varying quantities had limitless possibilities.

This kind of toy in the hands of a practical joker could wreck more than one beautiful friendship. What a reddish lavender light would do to a chartreuse dress, for instance, is beyond imagining. And if the lady in chartreuse happened to be the boss's wife, it would be just too bad.

Silly as this may sound, there is the germ of a real idea here. In a living-room it might be desirable to vary the over-all color within certain limits, because in this room the atmosphere will shift all the way from maudlin to meditative, and changing the color as well as the intensity of the lighting could be useful either in heightening the mood or suppressing it. The effectiveness of lighting and color is not to be sniffed at. We all know what the ruddy glow of firelight does to the mood of a group. The designers of the Palace of the Soviets in Moscow have planned to use changing color to help regulate the

Adjustable reading lamp from Sweden

53

speed with which crowds will move through its vast halls and corridors. And for a father interested in locating someone to take over the support of his daughter, a lighting installation using some color might work wonders.

THE COST OF COMPLETE LIGHTING

Quality in a house or a car or a suit of clothes costs money. The same is true for lighting. And any prospective builder who studies this as a separate budget item will not be too happy when he sees the figures. One reason the cost will seem high is that people have always spent much too little on lighting. When a family installs a bath, it demands high-quality fixtures, pipes that will last forever, and faucets that won't leak all the time. The difference between the middle-class bath and that in a rich man's house is, therefore, pretty much a matter of trimmings. But lighting design for the home has never gotten beyond the stage of so many outlets per room and a few sockets in the walls and ceilings. Thus, to bring lighting up to snuff—forgetting the lights in the bureau drawers, etc.—will cost more than people have been in the habit of spending.

Against this can be balanced intelligent planning and wisely selected equipment. Houses are full of lamps that cost from twenty to sixty dollars, which, as illuminating devices, are good for very little. Hall and dining-room fixtures are often purchased on the basis of looks and snob appeal, which results in a considerable waste of money. One of the best hall lights we have ever seen consisted of a swivel socket in a ceiling outlet, an aluminum reflector, and a 60-watt bulb. The total cost was under $1.75. There are ways of saving money in lighting as well as spending it.

It is not the function of this book to establish budgets, nor to replace the many product catalogues which manufacturers put out. It is our function to outline procedures and to present ideas. Nowhere is procedure more important than in home lighting. It is definitely not an amateur operation. In working out illumination patterns, the modern-minded architect will be invaluable, for he has been forced time and again to seek good solutions that will fit within his clients' restricted budgets, and his ingenuity is considerable. You will need him, anyway, for the planning and designing of the house—use him for the lighting as well!

DINING AND
ENTERTAINMENT

Simplicity is the keynote of this modern dining
room from a vacation house in Maine. All of the
materials were chosen for low first cost and ease of
maintenance, but they have been combined so
adroitly that the total effect is of richness and
warmth. Notice also the way the horizontally
sliding doors and windows extend all the way to
the ceiling. This detail, a favorite with modern architects, improves appearance, lighting and ventilation.

41

42

43

44

45

In the open plan, as pioneered by architect Frank Lloyd Wright (who designed the room shown on this page), the dining area is often a part of the living room—simply a planned space set aside for the table and chairs. In this instance the kitchen also opens into the main room by way of open shelving above the sink and a Dutch door, a sociable arrangement for the servantless house. The dining facilities shown on the facing page include a completely separate room set aside for eating (41), an alcove with one side open to the living room (42), and a space separated from the living area by a cabinet-partition, but not equipped with a door (43).

57

46

47

48

49

50

51

Even the most conservative homebuilder is usually willing to admit the desirability of a generous window in the dining space, and contemporary architecture, which has made large windows its trademark, rarely fails to satisfy this universal desire. In all of the rooms shown here, the windows extend the entire width of the outside wall, and in two-thirds of the cases, from floor to ceiling as well. Two of the rooms (46 and 47) employ large panes of fixed plate glass set directly in the frame, relying on smaller sash, or doors, for ventilation. Two more (49 and 51) have floor-to-ceiling sash that can be folded back out of the way in fine weather, leaving the wall entirely open. The other two (48 and 50) use smaller units of glass set in a grid frame.

52

53

54

55

56

Where the dining space is part of—or open to—the living room there naturally are occasions when it is desirable that it be closed off at least temporarily. There are a great many ways to accomplish this, but one of the simplest and handsomest we have yet seen is illustrated in view 53. This is a woven wood curtain (similar to the familiar porch awning material but turned on end) hung from a flexible aluminum curtain track attached directly to the ceiling. Other effective methods include conventional curtains (52), folding, floor-to-ceiling doors (56) and the patented, metal-frame curtain shown in 54 and 55, which is lined with felt and almost as good a sound-deadener as a partition.

57

58

59

Once freed from stylistic restrictions, the problem of providing space for dining is susceptible of almost as many solutions as there are houses to build and people to build them. The dining area may be set off by a partial partition topped with glass panels, as in 57; it may be combined with a porch cut out of the corner of the living room, as in 58 and 59; it may be so surrounded with windows as virtually to become such a porch itself, as in 60. Or, as shown in 61, it may be one of an articulated series of spaces sharing a continuous window but separated by storage units extending part way to the wall.

60

61

62

63

66

64

65

67

It is in the modest house that the modern approach to dining pays its biggest dividends: almost any nook or off-set in the plan offers sufficient space, if properly handled, for an adequate, attractive dining arrangement—one which does not necessitate the fuss and bother of unfolding a table and collecting chairs for every meal, and yet does not require an entire room to go unused between meals. A prime requisite—which has been satisfied in all of the examples shown—is that the dining place be pleasant, with a good-sized window and if possible, an attractive outlook. For this reason a bay window, like that shown in 64, is almost ideal, although the same effect can be achieved by other irregularities in the plan, as in 67. In view 66, the dining area is set off by a plywood panel which serves to shield the outside entrance to the room.

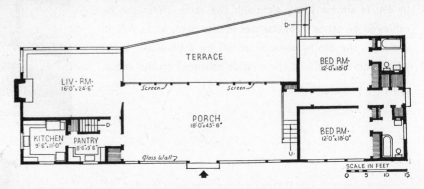

TERRACE

LIV·RM·
16'-0"x 24'-6"

Screen

Screen

BED RM·
12'-0"x18'-0"

D·

PORCH
18'-0"x 45'-6"

BED RM·
12'-0"x 18'-0"

KITCHEN
9'-6"x 11'-0"

PANTRY
8'-6"x 9'-6"

D·

U·

Glass Wall

SCALE IN FEET
0   5   10   15

69

This glazed recreation porch, which connects two halves of a divided house in California, shows how much sheer space can contribute to modern living. Little more costly than an ordinary porch, it provides ample indoor room for games and parties, and made possible a plan in which the balance of the rooms were compact and economical, since further provision for entertainment was unnecessary.

70

71

72

73

74

Living outdoors—and partially outdoors—is one of the major pleasures of owning a modern house. Modern heating methods and structural techniques which have made possible the window wall and glazed, horizontally-sliding doors have created entirely new types of rooms, as well as an entirely new relationship between the house and its site. Some of the possibilities are illustrated here: a dining porch in Michigan (70); a glazed wall in the rigorous climate of northern Pennsylvania (72); a dining space, half porch, half room, from California (71). The porch in 73, used for games and entertaining, is enclosed on one side by a glazed windscreen, open on the other for fresh air and unobstructed view.

CHAPTER SIX

THE WORK CENTER

THE OLD SAYING that there is nothing new under the sun, like so many old sayings, has a moderate amount of truth in it, and anyone looking for arguments to prove its truth can find ammunition in what has been happening to the kitchen during the past fifty years. Most people in America look back to a childhood in which much time was spent in a kitchen quite different from the room called by the same name today. For one thing, the old kitchen was big. For another, it was not merely a place where cooking was done. It was the work center of the home and it was also a social center. Here, by the stove, children were bathed, food was canned, laundry was done, and meals were eaten. In the evening people sat in rockers by the big, round table and read, sewed, studied, played games, and talked. The kitchen was the heart of the home.

In recent years the kitchen, like other parts of the house, has shown an extraordinary tendency to shrink. Enthusiasts for the "minimum" kitchen pointed out that several hundred people could be provided with complete meals from a dining-car kitchen so small that you could hardly turn around in it. The efficiency boys counted the number of seconds it took the housewife to get from here to there, the inches to the flour can, the steps from the refrigerator to the stove and back again. Their dream was a kind of circular closet where the house wife stood in the center and reached for everything without moving. They never got quite that far, which is just as well, but they did get awfully close

to it, which was not. Efficiency in the home and the well-being of the housewife depend on more factors than steps and minutes.

For one thing, the housewife is not a chef on a Pullman diner. She does not have to feed two hundred people a day. And the chef, lucky fellow, does not have to make beds, run to answer the door, or keep two or three children under control while he is cooking. Moreover, as the kitchen shrank to the point where it was virtually impossible to get a dining table in it, it simply meant that the steps saved in preparing meals were more than made up for by the necessity to get dishes to the distant table and back to the sink again. If this was efficiency, it was a very strange kind.

Then there was the question of laundry. There was no room for it in the minimum kitchen. For families that had a laundress it didn't matter too

much if the equipment was down in the basement, but it mattered a great deal if the laundry was another of the housewife's jobs. Have you ever tried starting a meal in the kitchen, starting a wash in the cellar, running up once to see what the children were doing, a second time to answer the phone, and a ninth or tenth time to take care of some other upstairs chore? And have you ever met anyone who enjoyed the discomfort of working in a damp, badly lighted space? Maybe hauling sixty pounds of wet clothes from the basement to the drying yard was good for mother's figure. The chances are, she would have preferred to meet this problem in some other way.

This does not mean there are no reasons for having a basement laundry. A recent survey made in one of the big war housing projects showed that tenants were about evenly divided in their opinions on this point. Those in favor of keeping the laundry underground had two reasons for this preference—one was that they did not like the mess laundry makes in the kitchen; and the other was that clothes could be dried in a pinch downstairs if it was raining. There are answers to both these arguments, however. One is that if the tenants had complete work centers instead of oversized closets labeled kitchens, doing the laundry would not make a mess. But a far more important answer is that equipment is rapidly getting to this point—in fact, some of it has been designed—where the washer, dryer, and ironer take up a phenomenally small amount of space. The increasingly popular first-floor heater room, incidentally, would be an excellent place for drying clothes if it were planned with this in mind.

There is another potent force which is doing a great deal to swell the kitchen to its old proportions —that is, the servant problem. Very few families, percentagewise, have ever been able to afford hired help. Servants, as a group, are disappearing. World War I took women out of domestic occupations

72

and put them into offices. World War II took a vastly greater number and put them into factories. The middle-class families and the rich, thrown more and more on their own resources, have been casting a jaundiced eye on the minimum kitchen.

WORK CENTER—SOCIAL CENTER

The modern kitchen cannot be a small room. It must be a big room—possibly the biggest room in the whole house. It should contain all the cooking facilities, all the laundry equipment, probably the heater, and certainly all necessary space and facilities for family meals and even meals when guests are present.

You will remember that a while back we talked about the kitchen-living room, an idea which has steadily gained in popularity. This is merely an expansion of the work center idea. Advocating this kind of planning doesn't mean that it would make sense for every American family to start doing everything in the kitchen. It certainly does not mean that dining under all circumstances has to go on next to the sink. But it must be emphasized that if families who do their own work are going to reduce the mechanics of living to the minimum, this scheme has a great deal to be said for it. If you can afford a kitchen work center plus a dining-room and a living-room, well and good. But unless you are in the top income group, you won't be able to afford all of them. This is the main argument for the work center. The housewife spends a disproportionate amount of her time working around the kitchen, and there is every reason why this room should be designed to be a completely livable, as well as workable, interior.

One of the great inventions of the thirties was the so-called streamlined kitchen. It was full of cabinets which stuck out a uniform distance from the wall and below-counter cupboards which made it difficult or impossible to sit comfortably on a stool

The old kitchen was big—

while you worked. The streamlined kitchen was sold in the name of efficiency and good looks, and it was made this way because it was easy to manufacture. It was an improvement, but it was by no means a complete solution. Food preparation requires, among other things, the provision of working surfaces at different heights. Some operations can best be performed standing up, others sitting down. And if you sit down, there has to be some way of getting your knees under the counter. The streamlined kitchen, unless it included a planning desk or an old-fashioned table in the middle, offered no such conveniences.

There were other faults in this de luxe interior. The refrigerator was—and still is, for that matter—a bulky, clumsy box, poorly adapted to most types of storage and exceedingly wasteful of power. Getting at one small item meant holding a big door open while quantities of expensively cooled air spilled out. The present day stove, in which the broiler and oven are practically down at the floor, is another example of equipment which in some respects is worse than the models sold twenty years ago.

The ideal stove and refrigerator have been attempted time and again by designers, but they have yet to be put into production. Ultimately we will be able to buy packaged kitchen units which include refrigerators broken up into three or even more separate compartments, and stoves which have broilers and ovens at working height. Unfortunately we cannot wait for "ultimately."

However, there is one weakness in the streamlined kitchen we can do something about. That is the disposition and design of the storage cabinets. By building a ring of over-counter cabinets all around the room we get a considerable amount of well-located storage space. Unfortunately, the windows suffer. Some architects have tried to solve this by putting glass above and below the cabinets. But a far more attractive and workable approach would be to take all the cabinets off the main window wall and put them elsewhere. There could be a storage wall (see Chapter XII) on one side of the kitchen. Running from floor to ceiling, it would have adjustable shelves like the existing cabinets, but it would have far more of them than we are accustomed to. It would also provide the shallow storage space which is so desperately needed. Cans, bottles, glasses, and small packages of food should not be stacked three deep or, for that matter, two deep. An irritating operation performed in any kitchen (it would probably be more accurate to say, in every kitchen) is the endless business of taking down everything at the front of a shelf to find something sitting at the back. No millennium is needed to remedy this; if your architect works out a suitable design, any mill or even a good carpenter can build it. One trick is the arrangement similar to the one we have on refrigerators, where the door itself contains some of the shelving. It would be no trouble at all to build some storage cabinets so that half of each shelf is on the door and the rest in the unit itself.

DESIGNING THE COOKING AREA

There seem to be only three general plans for the arrangement of cooking equipment and the accompanying fixtures. There are the U, the L, and the straight-line plan. We have seen examples of all three types in kitchen work centers. Since they all seem to have advantages, it would be difficult to recommend one over the other two. With the U, for example, one leg sticks out into the middle of the room. In many ways this is excellent. If the sink is put into the projecting leg, it means that dishes can be taken directly from the table to the sink without going into the cooking area itself. The U scheme also tends to segregate the cooking operation—which has its points.

The L, on the other hand, because it follows two walls of the room, leaves more open space in the middle, which again has its advantages. The straight-line set-up has the outstanding virtue of being the least conspicuous, because once the dishes are put away the entire room becomes available for other purposes. On this point you will have to make up your own mind. The arrangement should be related to family habits and personal preferences and

74

a pat solution which will work equally well for everybody cannot be developed.

EQUIPMENT

When we think of a kitchen, we think of three items: sink, stove, and refrigerator. The work center, however, has a lot more than three items. It would be wise to plan for possible additions. For one thing, it will almost inevitably have a quick-freeze unit—which will finally be reduced to compact, cabinet size. It will also contain the laundry equipment, which, as we have seen, is also shrinking to manageable proportions. The rapid improvement in dish-washing machines, some of which will also dry the dishes (this has been a standard arrangement in many restaurants for some years) means that more and more people will consider them necessary rather than luxury items. The same is true of that wonderful gadget which disposes of garbage by grinding it up and flushing it away.

We have here, incidentally, still another reason for increasing the size of the kitchen. The old kitchen simply isn't big enough, anyway, if these additional items are going to be included. But let us not assume that new equipment is the whole story. The greater the number of things, the more important the planning. If the room is so arranged that traffic through it and work in it conflict at any point, the room is no good. You can't have a laundry, no matter how efficient, if it interferes with food preparation because it isn't in the right place. The same is true of the placing of storage units. And the same is true of the dining furniture.

THE HEATER

The house described all through this book is a basementless house. The main reasons for leaving out the basement are described in Chapter XII. Such a house works only if equivalent space is provided above ground. This is particularly true of the fur-

more like about 33% (will give equiv. efficiency.)

nace. It used to be necessary to keep the heater in the cellar because most systems worked on gravity. Heat rose to the rooms above by convection, whether air, steam, or hot water was used, and it fell again, thus completing a cycle. Most plants today, however, are of the forced circulation type—that is, they use a fan where air is the medium and a pump where water does the job. This removes the original reason for keeping the furnace in the basement. The gradual shift in fuels is the other reason.

It would be possible to put the furnace in a separate room somewhere on the ground floor, but it would be equally possible to put it into a kind of closet opening off the kitchen. We are assuming here that the furnace will use either gas or oil. For coal, even stoker-fired coal, much more space will be required. But if one of the compact new plants can be installed in a closet off the kitchen, it has one tremendous advantage, and that is, that the kitchen itself contains the space which any heater needs to have around it for inspection or repair. The saving of space to be achieved in this manner —by eliminating the cellar—is worth making.

PICTURE OF A WORK CENTER

Let us now try to imagine what the room itself might be like. It has one or more big picture win-

dows, because storage cupboards have been grouped in such a way that picture windows could be used. It has a fan and duct which keep out most of the soot and grease. It probably has an acoustically treated ceiling and a resilient floor. If the architect has been intelligent in his approach, the room is completely free from its familiar hospital operating-room atmosphere, thanks to the incorporation of natural wood surfaces, bright color, and fabrics. The wall adjoining the dining space is movable, opening perhaps on the play yard, which might also serve as a convenient dining terrace. The lighting is wonderfully flexible. There is local illumination for the work surfaces, direct light for the dining table, and soft, general illumination which can give this room the same air of livability as the living-room itself. If it functions for a good part of the day as a playroom, it contains cupboards for toys and games. It works beautifully for a large number of household tasks, and it looks so well that you would be glad to entertain in it, too.

A short while ago we described the work center to a friend of ours. She listened quietly at first, then with growing excitement. Finally she interrupted, "I could *work* in that kind of a room!" Of course she could! But that's not what we're driving at. The point is, she could really live in it.

75

CHAPTER SEVEN

THE ROOM WITH-OUT A NAME

A FEW MONTHS ago a young architect who worked in Washington wandered into our office to pass the time of day and exchange whatever bits of news there might be. It was obvious, however, that he had something else on his mind. We waited. Pretty soon out it came, along with a fat black pencil. Paper was found and shoved under the pencil. Architects, as you may have heard, are very fond of flavoring talk with drawing. Again we waited.

"Want to see the perfect house plan?" he asked finally. He smiled apologetically, but we didn't. Our visitor was one of the most brilliant architects in the country, and his ideas always made sense and were frequently inspired.

"Sure we want to see the perfect house plan. Let's have it!"

"Well,"—he began drawing—"you start with a living-room. Only it isn't really a living-room. Too small. It has room for only four or six people, and

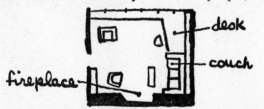

the walls are covered with built-in bookshelves, desk, etc. Guess you might call it a study, or parlor, or maybe a kind of retiring room. Parents might use it to get away from the kids."

76

This was a little disappointing. "So what?" we asked. "We've seen studies before."

"I'm not through"—still drawing. "Next to it there is a small kitchen, cooking on one side, dining on the other."

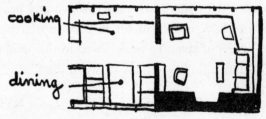

"Well?"

"Well," he continued, "between this kitchen and a third room there is no partition, or maybe just a glass partition. The third room is big. Biggest room in the house."

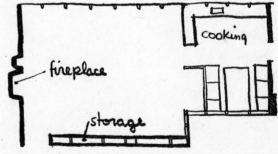

"It does look big," we conceded. "What happens there?"

"Everything, practically. Ping-pong, bridge, movies, dancing. The children can play there. Or you could cook in the fireplace. Good place for a dinner party, too."

"What do you call it?"

"I don't know," he said, puzzled. "I was going to call it the 'dirty room' because the materials would be practically indestructible, and the kids could make any kind of mess without doing any damage. But that's not a very good name. It would be pretty swell-looking when it was fixed up."

"It doesn't look like much of a plan to me," one of us snorted. "Where's the entrance? Where are the bedrooms?"

"Wherever you want to put them," he retorted. "And it isn't a plan, anyway—it's a diagram."

"And what makes it the perfect plan?"

He looked up from the drawing, surprised. "Why, the big room, of course. The room without a name."

A few days later another architect walked in. He had come in from the West Coast by way of Brazil and points north. For some reason or other, the talk again turned to houses. Our West Coast visitor also had a house on his mind. And his house, too, had a big room—in fact, leaving the bedrooms out, all it seemed to be was a big room.

There were only two partitions in the main living area: a light screen wall for the kitchen, and a heavier barrier that set aside a study, space for reading, or just privacy. This latter consisted of bookshelves that did not reach the ceiling.

This seemed to be too good to be a coincidence.

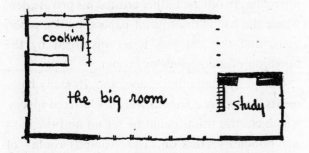

Had he seen the first plan? No, he hadn't. He had been mulling over the idea for quite a long time. Looked like the kind of house one might want for oneself.

"Funny," he said, looking at the sketch our friend from Washington had made.

"Yes," we agreed, "it is funny."

Less than a week after this a man came in from Detroit. He was not a house architect at all, but a member of a big office specializing in industrial plants and office buildings. But he couldn't talk anything but houses because he had just purchased a piece of land and was going to build himself one.

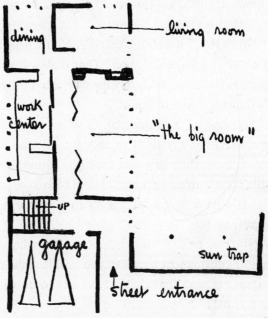

Would we like to see the house? Yes, we would like to see the house. Out came the pencil.

Many features of the house were unusual, because of special consideration given to the view and the sun. But a couple of things immediately attracted our attention.

"What's that?" we asked, pointing to a small square at the back of the plan.

"That's the living-room. Good place for it, don't you think? No street noises."

"Sure," we replied. "But it's tiny. You couldn't get more than a half dozen people into it without a shoehorn."

"That's true," he admitted. "I guess you shouldn't really call it a living-room. It's more a kind of study or parlor, I suppose. My wife and I wanted it because we thought it would be a good idea to have one room where we could shut the door and have a little privacy once in a while. Anyway, we have a big room for parties and for the kids."

Yes, he had the "big room" right across from the kitchen. It even had folding doors along the side to make it bigger. We told him about the architect from Washington and the architect from the West Coast. He looked crestfallen, but also pleased that he was traveling in such high-powered company. "Damn it all!" He grinned. "I thought I had an original idea for once."

"Don't fret," we said. "You did. You worked it up on your own, didn't you? That makes it original enough for anybody. By the way, what do you call that big room of yours?"

"You know," he confessed, "I've been wondering about that myself. I've thought of several—you've heard them all—but they don't quite seem to fit. The room's functions are kind of mixed, anyway. It's hard to describe them in a word. Any suggestions?"

"No," we said. "No suggestions. But what we want to know is why are all of you people suddenly designing houses that always have one room without a name?"

No, we did not invent these stories. The conversations took place in exactly the order we have related them. What is more, other architects have since come around with variations on the same theme. Why? We aren't sure why this is happening in so many different places at the same time, but we have an idea.

A FLAW IN THE HOUSE

Contemporary houses have been planned to provide an acceptable minimum of living facilities within an absolute minimum of space. In playing this game, architects and builders took the living-room, bedrooms, kitchen, and bath, and worked them over and over until the last "wasted" square

inch had been extracted. "Living-room, dining-room, kitchen, and bedroom" became a set formula which was supposed to provide all the living space the average family needed. The only trouble with the formula was that it ignored living. But people don't forget about living, no matter what the smart speculative builders and the routine-minded architects say.

People, praise God, don't stay put in pigeonholes, no matter how the compartments are labeled. And, because they are neither animals nor machines, they end up by demanding space for activities that don't fit into the pigeonholes, although nobody seems to be able to find a suitable name for that space. The purposes and potentialities of the space are too indefinite to label as yet, but they are none the less real.

Our "room without a name" is not entirely new. Many houses used to have something like it. Do you remember the houses of the seventies and eighties that had towers growing out of a tangle of roofs? Generally absurd in size and shape, the towers were always picturesque. The funny little cut-up rooms inside were the exciting property of the children, who used them for everything from playing steamboat captain to hiding from imaginary enemies. Such leftover rooms, however, were not always for the children alone. In some of the more accessible rooms Mother kept her sewing things and odd assortments of household paraphernalia. In others, Father created his private den, where the happy disorder of papers, books, pipes, guns, and the rest was never disturbed by the intrusion of a dustcloth or broom.

Old houses had other spaces, too. In many basements there were comparatively uncluttered spaces, where electric trains could be set up and the messier hobbies carried on. The "rumpus room" of more recent vintage extended these activities to include games, dancing, movies, and so on. Such a basement room, though more completely decorated, was still a makeshift or afterthought, and it was usually the unforeseen result of shifting from coal to a cleaner and less bulky fuel. Moreover, none of the basement playrooms covered the broad range of uses we are talking about.

Some people have already gone beyond the basement playroom in their houses. A striking example is a house built to sell for $20,000 in a Chicago suburban development. It has a ground-floor space called a recreation room, which is about as large as the living-room and is separated from it by a large sliding door. It can be reached from both front and back entrances without going through the living-room, and it is well equipped to serve the purposes of the "big room." The idea obviously had genuine appeal, for the house was sold in short order.

WHY HAVE A NEW ROOM?

There seem to be as many reasons for this kind of room as there are people. A successful woman editor of a New York magazine is planning to build a room without a name as an addition to her home. Connected to the house by a glassed-in passage, it will function partly as a greenhouse, partly as a breakfast and miscellaneous-purpose room. For any family interested in hothouse plants and flowers such a room would provide a fascinating background for living as well as space for its hobby.

The greenhouse idea suggests any number of other hobbies which might be served by such a room. Properly designed, it might take care of messy ones, such as indoor gardening, carpentry, model building, metal working, painting, and the like; or others, such as music, which require only space for their full enjoyment. It is in connection with the noisy and dust-producing activities like the use of a power saw, however, that the advantages of the room are most effectively demonstrated.

On closer examination the room without a name shows a number of definite characteristics. An important one is that it is totally lacking in privacy.

Any member of the family may use it, and for practically any purpose. Since a major complaint about the house as it is now planned is the lack of privacy, it is interesting to see a room appear which insists on its "public" nature. We would not be entirely correct in concluding that this is just the living-room function slightly revamped, for the living-room traditionally has been set aside for the adults, and for a limited number of activities.

There is another interesting point about this room: it marks the first time a room *for the whole family* has appeared in the home since the days of the farmhouse kitchen. Coming at a time when the family is less tied to the home than ever before in its history, this fact presents something of a contradiction. "For the family," by the way, doesn't mean that all rooms in today's houses are specifically limited to certain members; we are merely pointing out that the "big room" is *intentionally* set up to cover the family's social and recreational needs, and that the usual adults-versus-children distinction has been abandoned.

A third idea also presents itself. By frankly developing a room which is entirely "public" as far as the family and its guests are concerned, *privacy is made possible*. Because there is an "extra room," the other living space can really be enjoyed in peace and quiet. The children's rooms, too, are no longer under the same pressure to double as playrooms and sleeping-study spaces.

These three ideas combine to produce a picture of a need and a trend. The need is clear enough: a house must be planned to meet adequately a normal family's requirements of both privacy and joint activity. It need hardly be mentioned that a "normal" family's requirements are by no means standardized. Some families are sociable, others are less so. Some have their fun with lots of noise and a considerable expenditure of physical energy, while others have as good a time more quietly. The room without a name, therefore, cannot follow any stock design or stereotyped arrangement; it is far too intimate an expression of a family's tastes. In spite of this, the room does seem to have certain standard features. Its furnishings and materials are definitely on the "tough" side, designed and selected to stand up under extremely hard usage. In all probability it will not include anything that might be damaged by dirt or dust, and it should be easy to clean. Since it will, on occasion, serve for entertainment of a fairly formal kind, it will have to have storage cupboards where toys, games, and tools can be kept out of sight. What furniture there is would tend to be built-in, or light in weight and highly mobile. None of these characteristics, incidentally, prevents the big room from being a very handsome one.

Granting the need, the actual trend is less clear. Can it mean that people are insisting more and more on living their lives in the way they want to? That they are more concerned with this than with impressing the neighbors? The present-day living-room, as we well know, is something of a "front." This is where guests are entertained; here we generally find the best furniture, the most expensive carpet, and the least evidence of normal family disorder. For these very reasons its uses are limited. Anything that might damage the furniture or disrupt the orderly arrangement is taboo. There are families to whom this does not apply, of course, but in general the picture seems fairly accurate. Can it be that the living-room is going the way of the old-fashioned parlor—or more properly, is it turning into a special-purpose room like the study? Will its functions be divided in the future between the small, quiet retreat and the big room? Possibly. Certainly the idea has much to commend it.

Other questions of a broader social character suggest themselves. We have all read articles about the family—its difficulties in the world of today,

the inadequacies of parents, the waywardness of children. Could the room without a name be evidence of a growing desire to provide a framework within which the members of a family will be better equipped to enjoy each other on the basis of mutual respect and affection? Might it thus indicate a deep-seated urge to reassert the validity of the family by providing a better design for living? We should like very much to think so, and if there is any truth in this assumption, our search for a name is ended—we should simply call it the "family room." As a matter of fact, even without social theories, it is still a very good and completely accurate name.

This much we do know: when a number of outstanding architects arrive almost simultaneously at the same planning idea, each being entirely ignorant of the others' activities, something is brewing. This "something" may not come to a head for many years, but it is a matter of experience that artists (this includes the best architects) reflect in an uncannily sensitive way currents in thought and design long before they are popularly accepted. What they seem to be anticipating now is a further development of the general living area of the house, a more freely organized arrangement of public and private spaces which would be closer to the actual needs of the modern family than anything that has been seen hitherto.

If this should prove to be the case—and none of us will know for some time whether it will or not— the validity of the underlying thesis of this book will have received confirmation from an unexpected quarter. The thesis, as we have outlined it, is that tomorrow's house needs no new inventions, materials, or techniques for its realization. What is required is a deeper understanding of today's trends, coupled with the most creative and bold use of the techniques already at hand.

CHAPTER EIGHT

HEATING

As far as the home builder is concerned, there are two ways of looking at heating, and only two. One is to consider the equipment—the furnaces, boilers, ducts, radiators, controls, and all the other paraphernalia that go to make the modern heating plant what it is. The other is to think of heating in terms of bodily comfort and health. Since very few of us are equipped to evaluate one piece of complex machinery as against another, and since we are concerned with the results and not with the means, we will look at heating from the second point of view.

There are certain pleasant experiences having to do with heating which everyone can recall. Most of us can remember the old-style kitchens of our parents or grandparents which had a great, black coal stove in one corner. And we can remember, too, the wonderful sensation of well-being produced by this stove on a cold winter's day. The big pot-bellied coal stove in the general store, which is still the social center of so many rural communities, produces the same agreeable effect. These experiences don't all occur indoors. Have you ever gone out on a chill, sunny day in spring or fall and noticed what a fine heating job the sun can do once you are in a protected corner out of the wind? Skiers are familiar with this even in midwinter, for it is possible to strip to the waist and still feel comfortable in the direct rays of the sun and those reflected from the snow. Most familiar of all, probably, is the experience of getting into bed in a cold bedroom and, after a brief tussle with frigid sheets, enjoying the extraordinary pleasure of breathing fresh, cool air while one's body is enveloped in the most delightful kind of warmth.

These examples—and we can think of others—have to do with heating, in spite of the fact that the "equipment" in one instance is one's own body, in another, the sun, and in a third, a stove. It is important to remember such experiences when thinking about heating, because all we are buying the machinery for is to duplicate in one manner or another these feelings of comfort.

HEATING IN YOUR OWN HOME

If you live in an average house, it probably consists of a number of separate rooms, all of which can be closed off from one another. It probably has two floors, sandwiched between a basement and an attic. Finally, the windows in relation to the total wall area are fairly small. You will recognize in this description, of course, a typical Colonial, English, or Victorian house. This kind of house is compact and easy to heat.

If you have a better-than-average heating plant, it furnishes automatic heat—that is, it runs on gas, oil, or stoked-fed coal, and has a thermostat which turns the furnace on or off depending on room temperature. Yet even with this plant, which represents many decades of patient experimentation by manufacturers, it is not difficult to recall occasions when something less than optimum comfort was produced. Frequently there are drafts. Heating is often sporadic and uneven. The air near the floor tends to be rather cool, and one of mother's major chores is to keep small children off it in cold weather. Also, the thermostat sometimes behaves in a strangely unreasonable manner. When it is set at 70° in the evening, the rooms may be too chilly for comfort. When it is set at 68° on a sunny day, the rooms facing south may be overheated. It may have other faults as well. If the system uses steam, the radiators are sometimes noisy, occasionally produce an unpleasant odor, and tend to soil the walls behind and above them. Also, people frequently complain that the rooms heated in this manner are stuffy.

HEATING IN THE MODERN HOUSE

The tendency in home building today is to move farther and farther away from the traditional old-style house. Survey after survey has shown that an increasing number of people are demanding houses on one floor. They don't care particularly whether they have basements or not. They like the idea of the "open plan," where living, dining, and even kitchen facilities are related rather freely to one another. In the newer plans partitions are omitted to gain a feeling of space, as many doors as possible are left out, except in rooms like bedrooms and baths where privacy is essential, and generally to simplify the whole living pattern within the house. This is equally true in expensive houses, where people can build all the enclosed rooms they want to, as well as in cheap ones, where it is necessary to eliminate such elements as the dining-room because the budget isn't large enough.

The modern house brings with it great advantages. That is why people are building more and more of them every year. It also brings very real problems. We all know that a house with insulated walls and few windows is easier to heat comfort-

ably than a house where entire walls may be made of plate glass. We can imagine, too, that if an open living space extended from the warm side of the house to the north where a cold wind might be blowing, there would be a measurable temperature difference at the two ends of this space, and warm and cold air currents would promptly be set up, creating drafts and all of the attendant discomforts.

When the first modern houses were built, their architects were aware of these new problems, and they tried in a variety of ways to solve them. One method they tried was to use radiators of special shapes. For instance, where a picture window extended almost the full width of the room, long row radiators were installed under the sills so that cold air falling away from the window surface would immediately hit the radiator. Where air conditioning was used, the typical register was replaced by long grilles which ran the full length of the window, the purpose being the same—to keep the cold air from getting into the room and causing discomfort. Nevertheless, when all of these things had been tried, it was found that air near the floor was still colder than it should be even with the thermostat pushed up to 76° or 78°. And in basementless houses where the floor was set directly on the ground or above a shallow unheated air space, the problem was very serious. Serious, that is, until the day when some nameless hero had an idea. A very good idea. He thought, "Why not let the floor be the radiator? A radiator so big could have a very low surface temperature. This would eliminate cold floors, and it might have other advantages."

THE RADIATING FLOOR

Young students of architecture who have to learn about buildings of many periods run into descriptions of the Roman bath—probably the most luxurious athletic club in the history of the world. In studying it, they find that the furnaces were underneath the rooms, and before the hot flue gases were allowed to escape through the chimneys, they passed through the hollow floors, thereby providing a very agreeable temperature inside. In Korea ages ago the houses of the noblemen generally had one room called the spring room, where they could escape the bone-chilling dampness of the Pacific winter. These rooms were heated in exactly the same way as the Roman baths. There was a little furnace, and underneath the floor there was a labyrinth through which all of the hot air had to pass before it got to the chimneys. These rooms did not have heating in our sense—they really had climate. And it was possible for the fortunate few to enjoy quite literally the pleasant freshness of spring by returning to the room that was set aside for this purpose.

When Frank Lloyd Wright went to Tokyo to build his world-famed Imperial Hotel, he knew about this ancient method of heating, and in the bathrooms he installed electric radiators under the floor—possibly the first large floor heating installation in modern times.

In Europe during the twenties and thirties "radiant heating," as it was called, began to be used rather widely. The heating elements were usually put in the ceiling instead of in the floors. However, for reasons which we will see presently, the exact location of the equipment did not make a great deal of difference.

HOW RADIANT HEATING WORKS

The most common system of installing radiant heating in American houses is to lay a concrete slab on the ground with coils of pipe underneath the slab. Through the pipes passes steam or hot water—the latter is preferred at the moment. When the furnace is turned on and the heated water begins to circulate through the coils, the slab above warms slowly until it reaches a temperature of about 85°. A surface at this temperature is barely

warm to the touch. Instead of radiators scattered through the house, we now find that a large part of the house itself has become the radiator.

This huge radiator is not a radiator at all in the conventional sense. To understand why, we have to make a brief but important digression. We have to find out how heat is transferred from one object to another. Those who can still remember high-school physics will probably find the story familiar.

HOW HEAT MOVES

Heat, the textbooks say, can be transferred in three ways: by conduction, convection, or radiation. A traffic policeman who must stand for hours out in the cold often uses a wood platform about three inches high. This prevents contact with the cold pavement, or, as we would put it, the transfer of heat from his feet to the pavement by conduction.

People are made uncomfortable by sitting on a cold stone fence or by leaning against a cold window. The method of transfer in each case is the same.

In the average living-room where steam or hot water radiators are installed, heat is not transferred by conduction at all but by convection.

Convection refers simply to the movement of currents—in this case, air currents—resulting from the fact that some currents are warmer than others. In the living-room the air touches the radiators, gets hot, and rises to the ceiling. Then the cooler air comes in to take the place of the warmed air, hits the radiators, is also warmed, and also rises. Eventually the air loses its heat, drops to the floor, and the cycle is repeated.

What we call radiators are therefore far more accurately described as convectors, and this, in fact, is what the heating engineer calls them. In a gravity-type warm air system (this is the old-fashioned kind), the convector is in the basement. It is the furnace itself. The cool air drops into the air jacket around the fire chamber, gets heated, rises in the ducts, and enters the rooms through the registers. True radiation, however, is quite a different matter.

Radiation is the third type of heat transfer, and the only one that can be made independently of a supporting medium. If this sounds like scientific jargon, consider one or two examples. Between us and the sun there are unimaginably vast spaces which contain no air at all. Yet the warmth from the sun covers this ninety-three million miles at the rate of almost two hundred thousand miles a second. This radiant heat emerges from the great clouds of incandescent gas that surround the sun, goes through the sub-zero temperatures of interstellar space, then through our own atmosphere, which is a sixty-mile blanket of air and water vapor, and it is still doing a pretty good job when it lands in your back yard.

This is the way a true radiator works. It shoots out heat at a prodigious rate of speed, and the transfer from the radiating surface to whatever is warmed has nothing whatever to do with the temperature of the air between. This was demonstrated in an extremely dramatic fashion by some experiments which were made over a period of about five years at the Pierce Hygiene Laboratory in New Haven, Connecticut.

THE COPPER ROOM

In the Pierce laboratory there is a booth which is made entirely of copper—walls, floors, and ceiling. Copper, like other metals, reflects radiant heat. Hidden in the corners of this booth are electric coils which can be switched on to provide almost any desired amount of heat. Through a duct opening into the booth hot or cold air can be passed, depending on what the experimenters are trying to find out.

In the course of the experiment in the copper room hundreds of people passed through it and described their sensations. These sensations, to put it mildly, were extraordinary. One series of people, for instance, sat around the room and complained

that they were uncomfortably hot. Yet the thermometer showed an air temperature of only 50°. Why were they hot? Because the copper walls were radiating a great deal of heat, almost as much as the body was losing to the surrounding cool air. The net heat loss, therefore, was less than we ordinarily need to remain comfortable.

The same subjects went into another room where the air was above heat-wave temperatures—say 120°—and yet these people felt cool. Again it was heat radiation that furnished the clue, for the walls of this room had been cooled down to the point where they could almost have been used for making ice cubes, and the hot air was not sufficient in this case to counteract the loss by direct radiation from the body to the frigid walls. Here the experimenters came across—in extreme form, to be sure—a common reason for discomfort in the average home.

THE INVISIBLE RADIATOR

Most everyone has heard of "cold 70°"—that is, a decidedly chilly condition in a room where the thermometer showed a temperature that should have been adequate for comfort. The explanation is not to be found in the heating plant but in the reactions of the body.

If you walk into your bedroom and ask how many radiators are in the room, and there happen to be two units, one under each window, you might think the answer would be two. But it isn't two. It is three. For you yourself are the third radiator. If the bedroom has large, cold window surfaces, or if the walls are uninsulated and therefore cold, your body will start radiating heat to the cold surfaces. And unless the air temperature is extremely high, you will lose more heat by radiation than you gain from the warm air. Here, we have a condition which is quite like that which the Pierce Foundation scientists set up artificially. If you insulate yourself rather than the walls, you will feel warm again. That is why, for example, we sleep comfortably under wool blankets in cold bedrooms. The history of clothing and bedding, incidentally, is one of those stories of things that were developed in a highly unscientific manner to produce technically admirable results. One piece of research, also carried out by the Pierce Foundation, is a particularly fascinating example of what clothing does.

THE AIR-CONDITIONED ARAB

In the course of some investigations of heating and its relation to hygiene, one of the Pierce scientists stumbled across a strange and baffling question: Why, in the hot, dry climate of North Africa, did the Arabs go around wrapped in garments made up of layer upon layer of fine white wool? An Eskimo, he reasoned, might have very good reasons for traveling about in this manner. But why an Arab?

The white explained itself very easily. White tends to reflect rather than absorb solar radiation; which is why we wear light-colored and white clothes in the summertime. But how explain the wool? Finally, after studying the problem very carefully, he came across the answer. The wool formed an insulation layer between the air on the outside and the air touching the body. Evaporation through the pores cooled the skin, and the temperature of the skin was therefore actually lower than it would have been if exposed to the intensely hot air of the desert regions. In other words, while the outdoor temperature might be 120° or more in the sun, the air between the wool clothing and the body might be 90° or less. This strange tale, a by-product of impersonal scientific research, has one instructive moral: heating cannot be considered solely in terms of equipment, since comfort is the object in view, and this may be influenced by a wide variety of factors, none of them having anything to do with furnaces or radiators.

RADIANT HEATING AGAIN

Where heating coils are used in the floor with perhaps supplementary coils imbedded in the walls or ceilings, the normal tendency of the body to radiate heat to cold surfaces is counteracted because most of the surfaces are warm. Some surfaces are warmed by the heating coils directly behind them. These, in turn, radiate heat not only to the body, but also to the walls, furniture, and other objects in the room. Presently these objects also become warm, and they, in turn, become radiators, though at a lower temperature than the primary source of heat.

THE ADVANTAGES OF RADIANT HEATING

We are all familiar with changing styles in American houses. We know about the Colonial dwellings of the seventeenth century, and how Colonial was given up in favor of a Greek revival in the early nineteenth century. This was followed by neo-Gothic, Victorian, and all the styles up to the present day. Less familiar, perhaps, are the changes in heating styles. From 1920 to 1930, for example, steam was the system in vogue. This was refined to become "vapor," which was nothing more than a steam system operating at less than atmospheric pressure; that is, the temperature of the steam in the radiators was lower and heating was easier to control. Hot water was used, but not very much, because it was rather sluggish in operation. When this disadvantage was overcome by using circulating pumps which forced the hot water through the pipes and radiators, the hot-water system began to compete with the better types of steam and vapor installations.

All these systems, however, took something of a beating when air conditioning came into vogue. All that this "air conditioning" amounted to was a redesign of the old hot air furnace, and the addition of a fan to push the air around, filters to keep dust from coming into the rooms, and a tray of water to keep the air from becoming too dry. True air-conditioning systems, which involve cooling as well as heating, have been confined, in the housing field at least, to the most expensive residences, for there is nothing cheap about them.

Now we have radiant heating coming up as a contender. What are its chances? We must ask this question because, after all, its use is still limited. There are probably no more than five or six hundred houses in the entire country which are kept warm in this manner, and this is a mighty small number compared to the twenty-odd million dwellings.

One big advantage of radiant heating is that there are no visible radiators. There are no chunks of cast iron or copper under the windows, no grilles or registers to disfigure the walls. In other words, the system as far as the housewife is concerned is completely out of the way, which is a very significant point when you have to do the dusting. Radiators not only catch the dust but also deposit dirt on the walls around them.

The second advantage is that the floor is warm. This means that instead of having to grab the baby off the floor, mother can dump him there, because it is the most comfortable place in the room, and also the safest as regards colds.

The third and outstanding advantage of radiant heating is its evenness. Tests made in a number of dwellings in an eastern city showed temperature differences between air at the floor and air at the ceiling running as high as 20°. One room, for example, had an air temperature at the ceiling running as high as 80°, while the air at the floor was only 64°. Others showed variations less extreme, but still with temperature differences of 10° to 15°. This means expense, since heat losses to the outside become very high when air temperatures move up to 80° or more, and creates drafts.

The radiant-heated house shows practically no variation between floor and ceiling temperatures and, if insulated reasonably well and weatherstripped, is almost completely free from drafts. For old people and invalids as well as for small children this condition is ideal.

"All this is very fine," we can hear you say, "but what about the cost? Won't any system which works such wonders be fabulously expensive?"

86

THE COST OF RADIANT HEATING

The answer, based on actual experience, is that radiant heating installations are comparable in cost to high-grade air-conditioning (without cooling) or hot-water systems. If the house is designed for radiant heating—that is, if it uses a floor slab laid directly on the ground—there is a saving in foundation costs; and this may in some cases make it actually cheaper than an old-fashioned heating system.

A major worry of most people confronted with the idea of radiant heating is that pipes, inextricably imbedded in rock under three or four inches of concrete, could become a terrible headache if they ever sprung a leak or broke or froze. These troubles, however, have not developed, because modern welding techniques and testing methods are pretty close to foolproof.

Is radiant heating, then, the complete answer to all our problems? It could be, in the opinion of many authorities, if other factors were present. One of the factors is house design. This kind of heating works at its best in a one-story house, although it has been successfully applied to those with two floors. Its demands in the way of insulation and double glazing are greater than those presented by other types of heating.

This emphatic recommendation of a kind of heating that is not particularly well known as yet does not discount by any means the certainty of further developments and further improvements in the years to come. The basic elements of heating, however, will remain precisely what they were in the days of the cavemen, for they stem directly and inescapably from the reactions of the human body to its physical environment.

Radiant heating by itself does not provide all the factors needed to control indoor climate. It does nothing about ventilation. It lacks air-conditioning's ability to clean and humidify incoming air. These problems, which can be met by separate equipment, are discussed in a subsequent chapter.

76

77

78

KITCHENS AND BATHS

There is a widespread notion that today's houses have about the most up-to-date kitchens and bathrooms imaginable. This is only partly true. Modern designers who have given the cooking and sanitation departments a fresh look have come up with all sorts of new ideas. One such is the modern version of the "old fashioned" service opening shown in 76 and 77. Besides opening the kitchen to the dining space, this puts the percolator and toaster within reach of the table, giving the master of the house something to do while he is waiting for his eggs.

79

all low storage

80

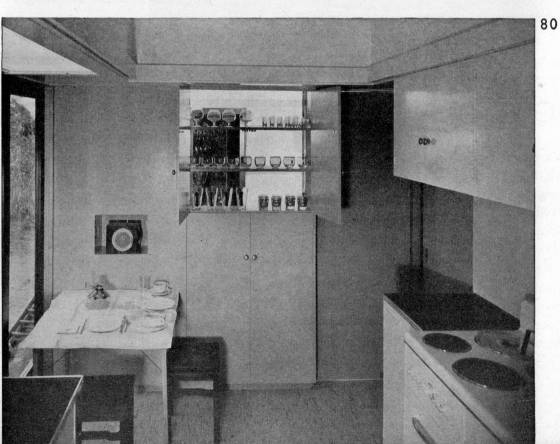

81

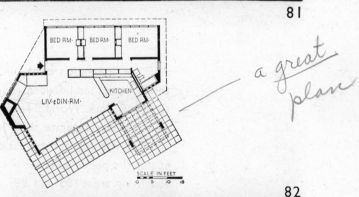

a great plan

82

A great many variations of the service-opening idea are possible, depending on just what you want to accomplish. The one used in 79, for example, is primarily intended for sliding trays of soiled dishes back into the kitchen, while picture 80 shows an entirely different approach: a two-way cupboard into which glassware is placed as it is washed at the sink, accessible from the dining room when setting the table. All such expedients, however, are simply compromises in comparison with the full-fledged living-kitchen shown in 81 and 82. In this arrangement cooking, eating and relaxation areas are merged in one attractive space, divided only by a waist-high bar. Ideal for servantless living, this scheme is both sociable and convenient, saves space and construction dollars.

83

84

Another illustration of the living-kitchen scheme, this series of semi-divided rooms was exhibited at the New York World's Fair. Its carefully studied plan provides separate sinks for food preparation and dish washing, and a great deal of storage space at just the points where it is most useful. Cooking and living areas (83 and 85) are divided by open shelving for glassware. An important feature of the design, basic to the whole living-kitchen idea, is the use of rich, attractive materials throughout, so as to eliminate the aseptic atmosphere ordinarily associated with the separate kitchen. Natural wood cabinets, dark linoleum work surfaces, monel metal sinks and generous use of exposed brickwork all contribute to making the space pleasant to live in as well as work in, and equally attractive throughout.

85

86

87

91

88

89

90

91

92

Modern architects have developed a number of practical details to make the conventional kitchen a more convenient and cheerful workspace. A favorite with many designers is the introduction of narrow, horizontal windows between the work counter and wall cupboards, as in view 91. This is sometimes extended to include another row of sash in the useless space above the cupboards (92), and the same concern for better daylighting has led to various clerestory arrangements like those in 88 and 89. View 90 shows an excellent solution of the problem of the inaccessible space created where two work counters meet in a corner: revolving shelves which swing out when needed, disappear into the corner when not in use.

93

94

95

96

97

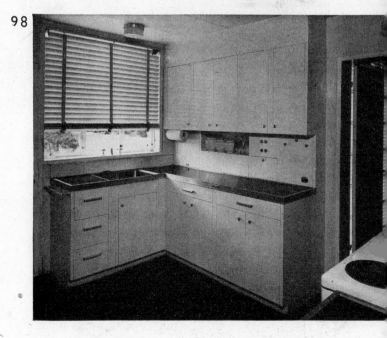

98

These designs come as close to the "dream house" category as anything you will find in this book. Views 93 and 94 show a full size model of an ideal kitchen developed by a glass manufacturer to stimulate use of his product and including redesigned, and so far unobtainable equipment. The one-piece, manufactured kitchen shown in 95, which has a drawer refrigerator instead of the usual type is actually in production but not yet in wide use. Pictures 96 and 97 show another one-piece unit, with bath and kitchen fixtures on opposite sides, from a much-publicized prefabricated house that is no longer manufactured. The basic idea, however, is being applied elsewhere.

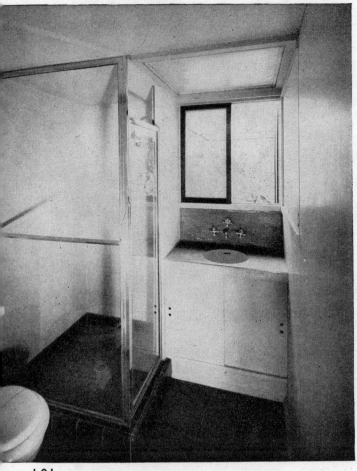

101

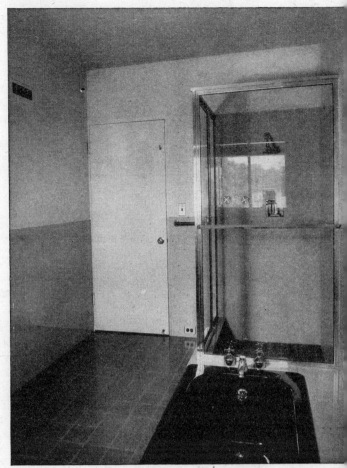

103

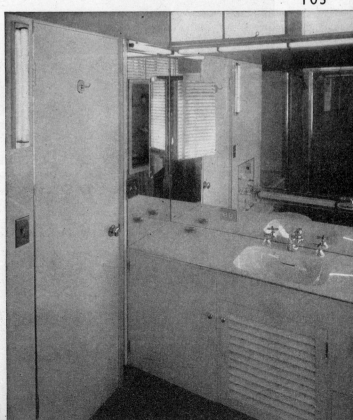

102

The stereotyped, porcelain-and-tile bathroom, supposedly the crowning glory of American civilization, has been the object of the same kind of reexamination the modern architects gave the kitchen, with equally exciting results. Putting aside the immutable law that bathroom windows must inevitably be too small for a self-respecting burglar they have, as in 99, set out to make the bath one of the pleasantest rooms in the house, and have even provided for amateur gardening, as in 100. A common feature is generous shelf space for the lavatory, two versions of which are shown in 101 and 103. Another popular device, which adds spaciousness to small rooms, is the glass shower enclosure used in 101 and 102.

104

105

106

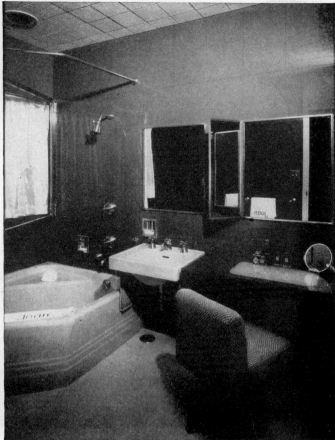

107

108

While these bathrooms are all of the luxury type, the design-approach they represent can be applied as easily to the modest house as to the mansion. Views 104 and 105 show a combination bath-dressing room with a continuous counter fitted with drawers for clothing and finished in wood veneers and plastic. The room shown in 106 and 107 has walls of structural glass, and an angle tub with a broad rim which serves as a seat. The translucent top of the dressing table is lit from below, providing illumination for the lower part of the face. View 108 shows a bath finished in natural wood and marble, and equipped with a counter lavatory very similar to those used in Victorian houses. Such materials are not much more expensive than the ones ordinarily employed in bathrooms, and are considerably more attractive.

109

110

111

112

113

Here are five versions of the counter lavatory, worked out in different materials and to fit various planning ideas. View 109 shows a recessed unit set in the wall of a bedroom and concealed, when not in use, by a swinging door. The counter in 109 is of varnished mahogany, and the fluted apron, made of half-round moldings, forms a cupboard for towels. Valves are controlled by foot pedals. View 111 shows an ingenious arrangement of shelving attached to the cupboard doors, view 112 a double lavatory, in marble, for a family bath. The unit shown in 113 is suitable for factory production, and shows how the counter-lavatory idea might be applied to a stock fixture. This one is located in the anteroom of a divided bath, with doors on either side leading to compartments for the tub and water closet.

CHAPTER NINE

BATHROOMS ARE OUT OF DATE

Generally a "luxury" approach

WHAT IS A bathroom?

"A bathroom," someone replies, "is a room containing a water closet, a lavatory, a tub, and maybe a shower."

How big is a bathroom?

"A bathroom," continues our informant, "is about five and a half feet wide by six feet long."

Why is it that size?

"That's easy," we are told. "These dimensions are about the smallest that will take the three required fixtures."

Oh! So the bathroom was designed for the fixtures. What about the people?

"I guess the builder didn't think about them."

That is what is wrong with bathrooms.

Now let's try again. What is a bathroom?

In the first place, it isn't necessarily a room at all. When plumbing was first installed in city houses, it went into the hall bedroom, which was about the only available place. In the seventy-odd years that followed, the bath has stayed the same old hall bedroom, slightly streamlined.

The functions served by the bathroom require plumbing fixtures, maneuvering space, counter area, good lighting, and adequate storage. For one person, or possibly two, there is no reason why these functions should not be performed in a single room. But for a family there are good reasons why they should not.

Some time ago one of us had the job of designing a very elaborate and expensive town house in New York City. The top floor was to be the owner's suite, with one large bedroom for himself—bath adjoining, of course—and across the hall another large bedroom, also with bath, to be used as a guest room. As the plans progressed the owner decided that somewhere on this floor he needed a third room which could be used part of the time as an office in the home, part of the time as a second guest room. This meant chopping one bedroom in half and somehow providing, in a now restricted area, bath facilities for not one bedroom but two.

This might have been solved, as it has been solved so frequently, by putting a bath between the two rooms. But it turned out to be impossible. If we had done this, there would have been practically no space left for beds in the sleeping rooms on either side.

The plan as it finally worked out is not a bathroom at all, but a string of separate compartments. Each bedroom has a separate lavatory with laundry hamper below the basin, installed in a shallow closet. The water closet has its own compartment with a door from each room. And, finally, there is a third space with a shower, also accessible from both rooms.

This system of breaking down the bathroom into its component elements can be worked with a great many variations. Where there are a number of bedrooms on one floor, for example, and there is no possibility of providing a bath for each room, the scheme of having a lavatory in each bedroom will work wonders in taking the pressure off the bathroom. It is possible to go to the other extreme, where space and funds are available, and convert the bath into a bath-dressing room whose amenities are vastly superior to those of the usual restricted space. But the main advantage of considering the bath not as a fixed room of a standard type is that it frees planning all through the sleeping area, can increase convenience at no increase in cost, and generally provides that flexibility so important in the house planned for living today.

THE THREE-PASSENGER BATH

The most spectacular example of the bath-in-compartments yet produced is a unit designed by Morris Ketchum, Jr. and Jedd Reisner for *Life* and *The Architectural Forum*. Created to meet the needs of a whole family, it is ingenious in plan and attractive in appearance.

The largest space in the bath is taken up by a lavatory and a mirrored storage compartment. The lavatory has foot controls for the faucet, a broad counter, and a generous cupboard below. Above is a medicine cabinet, in which the shelves are attached to the swinging mirrors.

104

Each of the other two fixtures which make up the bathroom has its own compartment and its own door, and the tub-shower compartment is sufficiently large for dressing as well as bathing. Now let's consider this bath as it would work in the average home.

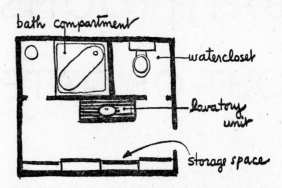

Whoever got up first might dash into the shower compartment, leaving the lavatory and water closet both free and private. If there were only one bath in the house, father might be shaving while mother was dressing and while the children were using the bathtub.

The Ketchum-Reisner bath has one serious disadvantage: it takes up a square space between three and four times as large as the minimum bathroom. The "three-passenger" principle, however, can be applied in less space and other shapes. It will work very well, for example, in a space about five and a half feet deep and fifteen feet long. In the typical modern house plan, which is long and rather narrow, such a shape fits very conveniently between a corridor and the north wall, leaving the

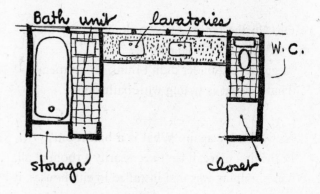

southern exposure for the bedrooms. All compartments, in this variant of the family bath, get outside light.

THE BEDROOM LAVATORY

To develop the idea a little further, let us assume that in addition to some such compartmentalized arrangement, two of the three bedrooms have built-in washbasins. These units, as we have already seen, can be compact, inconspicuous, and efficient. A space eighteen inches by thirty inches closed off by a door provides the needed facilities not only for washing, makeup, and shaving, but also for soiled linen. If these two built-in lavatories existed in addition to the bath, we would have a house where, without undue expense for plumbing, the various members of the family would never get in each other's way and almost all of the luxury of individual bathrooms could be enjoyed.

The bedroom lavatory is an item that could, and certainly should be, prefabricated. It should be possible, and perhaps it will be one of these days, to wander down to the local plumbing supply place and pick out one or two models which would be delivered complete with lights, laundry hamper, shelves, door, and so on. An ingenious manufacturer could work wonders with this unit. He could take a leaf out of the book of the Pullman car designers, for example. The familiar type of washbasin in sleeping cars that tilts up to become part of a wall cabinet is by no means beyond the capacity of a plumbing fixture manufacturer, and its advantage would be that the whole unit could then be made so thin that it would literally fit within the thickness of an oversized wall. Not even closet space would be required for its installation.

COUNTER SPACE

One of the most frequent complaints about the modern lavatory is that no matter where you put

the handbrush, hairbrush, toothbrush, or soap, it usually manages to slide down into the bowl.

There is a very simple way to eliminate this difficulty. It should be familiar to most of us, because the solution has been used in the kitchen for years. It consists of a flat-rimmed bowl set into a counter covered with rubber, linoleum, or some other resilient material.

This type of lavatory installation, of which a great many excellent examples can be found, must be considered in the planning, for the lavatory having such a counter must be given elbowroom and more. To be sure, this is another factor which tends to make bathroom space larger, but it is worth the extra space. The space underneath the counter can be used for shallow drawers, linen hamper, towel storage, and other items, such as extra soap, which should be kept in the bathroom.

Another source of occasional irritation, although a very minor one, is the necessity of having to twist faucets while one's hands are covered with slippery soap. This isn't a very serious matter, but there are devices on the market which will eliminate the faucets entirely if for any reason you would like to do so. These gadgets, rarely seen in houses, are regularly supplied to hospitals and other institutions where it is not only inconvenient for people to handle faucets but dangerous, since it might involve transmission of germs. There are two types: knee-operated and foot-operated. The latter sit on the floor and have pedals for hot and cold water.

Foot controls, like the double lavatories sometimes put into master bathrooms, are definitely in the luxury class, but fortunately there are people in this country who have the good sense to deny themselves necessities so they can enjoy luxuries.

Also in the class of luxury items is instantaneous circulating hot water, which involves the creation of a loop in the hot water supply line so that whether or not the hot water is being used, it is continuously circulating, though very slowly, through the pipes. This means that the moment the water is turned on, it runs hot. Most inexpensive of all the luxuries, and most satisfying, is an oversized supply pipe for the tub. If you have ever waited twenty minutes for the tub to fill up, the virtues of this item need no description.

The infra-red lamp is a gadget that has a great future in the American home once people become aware of its remarkable properties. Automobile and refrigerator manufacturers have used infra-red lamps for years in drying tunnels where car bodies and other freshly painted parts move through on conveyor belts. In the bathroom three or four dollars' worth of infra-red lamps could work wonders. That familiar chill when one steps out of the shower could be eliminated entirely by switching on one or two of these lamps, located in inconspicuous sockets on a wall or even in the ceiling. To produce a comparable feeling of well-being with conventional heating equipment, it would probably be necessary to heat the bathroom up to about ninety degrees, which of course would make it intolerable at all other times.

STORAGE

There is an entire chapter on storage which deals with the general problems of where to keep things. The special problems of the bathroom, however, are worth detailed discussion. The ideal bathroom —whether it's one room or in compartments— would have one feature on which agreement would certainly be unanimous. It would have room for all the towels ever used in it—in other words, it would have its own linen closet. It would have ample cupboards for the soap, toilet paper, infrequently used medicines, hot-water bottles, eyecups, and the host of miscellaneous items which somehow seem to get put away in two or three different closets in various parts of the house. Everything needed in the bathroom would be in the bathroom,

and there would be no need to race through chilly halls looking for things.

SHOWER VERSUS TUB

The most inexpensive and common expedient, of course, is to combine the shower and the tub in the same fixture. Where this is done, it is done rather badly, as a rule. Almost always there is a towel rack over the tub so that towels have to be removed if the shower is used. The curtain rod is a rather unattractive element in the room, and the curtains themselves are a nuisance. Furthermore, there is the inconvenience and danger of dancing around under an icy spray in anything as slippery and restricted as the average bathtub. The best solution, therefore, would be to separate these two items, even though additional space is required.

A stall shower does not need tile walls and chromium-plated trimming on a plate-glass door, desirable as these may be. It can be a space the size of a closet with walls made out of inexpensive asbestos sheets, or waterproof plywood covered with a good varnish. It can be one of the inexpensive prefabricated metal stalls which have been on the market for some years. The materials in the stall shower will range, therefore, from very cheap to very costly, and, whatever your budget, if you can afford a house you can probably afford one or another kind of shower installation.

In planning, two points should be considered carefully. A shower thirty inches square is usable but not very pleasant. If you can possibly do it, make it about four feet long by two and a half or three feet wide. This extra space will not make much difference in the size of the house, and it will turn a nasty little slot into a really luxurious place for bathing.

WALLS AND WINDOWS

We have already noted a certain dissatisfaction with the exceedingly unimaginative approach to

106

the planning of the sanitary facilities in the average bathroom. Equally striking to any architect concerned with building better houses is the really remarkable conventionality of the approach to the

high windows give light with privacy.

Good

design of this room. The windows are usually small in spite of the fact that the bathroom needs as much light as any other room and is entitled to just as good a view. And this tiny window, moreover, which invariably proclaims the location of the bath to the passer-by, is frequently set over the tub, where it is hard to reach, or over the water closet, where it produces a draft. It is true that privacy in this room is considered essential by the average homeowner, but there are many ways of getting privacy besides cutting down the window to the size of a porthole. One, if the view is no good, is to use translucent glass. Another is to keep the window high but at the same time to make it broad. Such a window extending from wall to wall and from the ceiling down to five feet above the floor will give ample privacy under almost any condition and at the same time transmit a great deal of useful light.

The attitude toward materials until now has been as restricted as the treatment of windows. Tile is run from the floor up to average elbow height, with painted plaster above. If the builder is very lavish, maybe the tile goes to the ceiling. But tile, for all its unquestioned merits, is not the only ma-

terial suitable for use in a bathroom. In a number of bathrooms which have been built in California houses redwood was used. Redwood, as you may know, like cedar and cypress, is filled with natural oils which give it a great advantage if it is located where it gets wet occasionally.

If the idea of a wood-paneled bathroom sounds strange to you, think about it a little while, and then see if it still sounds strange. There is no reason why the bathroom, just because it contains a few plumbing fixtures, should look like an operating-room on a battleship. If you like the idea of wood but don't want to use it in the form of planks, there is waterproof plywood. This material, made up of layers of veneer glued together with waterproof plastics, has been used very successfully on torpedo boats and airplanes. We can assure you, therefore, that you need have no qualms about its durability in your future bathroom.

Equally suitable are the flexible sheet materials, such as rubber and linoleum, which, as mentioned elsewhere, have desirable sound-deadening properties. They have the further advantage of bending around corners with the greatest of ease, so that a room sheathed with one of these finishes could have all round corners and be a lot easier to take care of. For that matter, round corners have long been used in tile baths and can be made of wood and metal as well.

LIGHTING

The critical point in lighting the bathroom centers on the lavatory. Here is the shaving mirror, and here, too, unless there is a separate dressing table, is where noses are powdered. Despite the fact that there are cabinets on the market which have built-in illumination and fixtures which will throw a great deal of light directly on the face, few people are thoroughly satisfied with the result. In a theater dressing-room, where good makeup is of vital importance, you will find that the mirror over

107

the dressing counter is completely surrounded with a ring of electric light bulbs. This may not be very pleasant, because the heat and glare from the brightly glowing bulbs are intense. But the idea is good, for the ring of lights gives even, shadowless illumination from above, from the sides, and, most important for shaving, from below.

Something of this kind has to be developed for the home lavatory, and it need not be unduly complicated. The simplest method, and the cheapest, involves the use of a single light over the mirror, plus the use of the white basin below as a reflector. Most basins are much too low for comfortable use, and if the lavatory were raised, its efficacy as a reflector would be increased. The single light need not be an incandescent bulb; it could perfectly well be a fluorescent tube. Still better would be the addition of two other lights on each side of the cabinet. Tube lights are much better in this location than incandescent bulbs, because the light would be spread over a bigger surface, and consequently there would be less discomfort from glare. What glare there is can be reduced further by the use of frosted glass or by hiding the bulbs and using curved reflectors of aluminum or stainless steel to direct the light to the face. An ideal solution, following the theater dressing-room example, would be to complete the ring and provide a light source from below as well. If you have an ingenious architect you will find that this solution is far from impossible. Perhaps some manufacturer will one day bring out such a unit. To date, however, it has not appeared, and if you want one it will have to be put together specially.

A few years back a demonstration house was built in New York City. It had an inside bath and therefore required full-time artificial lighting and ventilation. Instead of tacking up lights on the wall here and there, the architect, Edward Stone, made the entire ceiling a lighting fixture. The ceiling consisted of a grid of light wood bars about three inches deep, which made it look a little like an egg

108

crate. Above this there was a layer of frosted glass, and in the space above that were fluorescent tube lights. The grid directed all illumination downward, and the natural wood color softened and warmed the light, thus producing a really wonderful effect. In addition, there was local illumination on the lavatory mirror.

THE INSIDE BATH

In a single house it has usually been taken for granted that the bath will be located on an outside wall so that it will have its own window for daylight and ventilation. In big city apartment houses and particularly in large hotels, the reverse generally holds true, for land is so valuable and space so restricted that baths have to be buried in the core of the building to save valuable outside wall space.

Most people contemplating the building of a new house would probably reject the suggestion that they put one or more inside bathrooms in the plan, on the ground that such a bath is unpleasant to use and unhygienic. Nevertheless, they will think nothing of going to an expensive, up-to-date hotel where they will use the artificially lighted and ventilated inside bathroom without the slightest discomfort. In fact, they might even enjoy the unprecedented degree of privacy which this type of room affords.

When approaching the question of the inside bath, it is necessary, therefore, to distinguish between facts and prejudices, and between the real advantages and the real disadvantages of such an arrangement. It is true that in the great majority of houses there is frequently no particularly good reason why bathrooms should be removed from outside walls. There is usually all the perimeter needed for all of the rooms, and giving up ten or fifteen feet of exterior wall space for bathrooms does not create any shortage of such space. However, there are occasions when, by placing the bathroom within the core of the house, a considerable increase in planning flexibility can be achieved. This is particularly true when the bathroom is changed from its conventional form into a related series of compartments where the various functions are divided to give added usability.

There is another point about the inside bathroom that must be considered in evaluating its desirability, and that is, that in a one-story house or on the top floor, the inside bath can also be naturally lighted and ventilated by using clerestory windows or skylights. During the period of emergency war building a great many housing projects of a temporary nature built in various parts of the country used precisely this scheme. According to the few tenant surveys that were made, these bathrooms were well liked. Privacy was considered one advantage, while the added wall space, thanks to the elimination of the window, was another.

But war housing was not the first example of such planning in this country. Decades ago Frank Lloyd Wright, who seems to have had almost every good idea about houses some twenty years before anyone else, was building bathrooms and kitchens where the walls extended well above the roof so that light could be brought in from the sides. Wright has already emphasized the virtues of this scheme, not only for the reasons given above, but because, as he pointed out, kitchens with extra high ceilings and raised windows function in the same way as the large chimney—that is, general movement of air through the house would be set up, the high windows furnishing the outlet for the air. In a kitchen of this kind the problem of cooking odors is well on the way to solution, because air currents would be coming into the kitchen and passing out directly, carrying the odors with them. The same applies to the bathroom.

This is what *The Architectural Forum* has written about the inside bathroom: "One reason why inside bathrooms work better than those on outside walls is that they are usually better ventilated. Artificial ventilation insures a constant flow of air in one direction—that is, from other rooms into the bath, where objectionable odors are drawn off which otherwise might be distributed throughout the apartment. Mechanical ventilation establishes fixed constant ventilation not only of the bath, but cross-ventilation of other rooms. Because air is drawn from the rest of the apartment, the bathroom temperature remains fairly constant.

"Secondly, this ventilation works all the year round, whereas bathroom windows are frequently closed almost all winter. One cold blast of air is enough to keep the window closed for the remainder of a day, if not the season. Neither are city dwellers likely to leave a bathroom window open for long and let the soot sift in.

"The equipment in the inside bath may be economically arranged on one wall without blocking access to a window, as is often the case with the outside bath. This has been the cause of serious accidents, as the tenant may easily slip on a wet floor or tub when reaching over or stepping into the tub to open the window. Light from the small window is generally inadequate for either shaving or making up, and for this reason artificial light is preferred."

Use or rejection of the inside bath idea is a matter of personal taste. As far as that goes, so is the use of bath-in-compartments. What we have tried to show, and what is more important than the few new ideas discussed, is that the kind of thinking that produced the standard minimum bathroom is outdated, that an unprejudiced approach to one's living requirements can produce an astonishing variety of new and interesting solutions. Only a few years ago it was generally felt that the bathroom problem had been completely solved—that arranging three fixtures in a small area left little or no room for variations. We have seen that this is not the case. And there is a very good reason why it is the *modern* architect who has contributed the changes. It is because he forgets about the fixtures and remembers that he is designing for people.

CHAPTER TEN

MANUFACTURING

CLIMATE

A COUPLE OF weeks ago we helped a friend paint his kitchen. It had been a white kitchen to start with, and was getting a new coat of the same color. Except that it wasn't the same color at all. Wherever the new white went on the walls, the old white next to it suddenly turned a muddy yellow gray by contrast. Even the enameled electric clock, which had been faithfully scraped every month or two, seemed a rather dingy beige once the new paint surrounded it, and not the gleaming white everyone had imagined it to be.

This kitchen is in no way particularly remarkable. It isn't in the city, where soot discolors everything in sight, and it has been taken care of as well as a room could be. Yet after less than two years a high quality white paint was transformed into something just this side of mud.

What this leads up to is the observation that the activities in certain rooms produce their own "climate." The average kitchen, for example, is a Pittsburgh in miniature, where minute particles of soot from the cooking fire, burned food, and plain ordinary everyday grease get into the atmosphere and wander around the kitchen, and the adjacent rooms, too, until finally they land on the walls or furniture. In fact, laboratory analysis has disclosed that some of the fish mother fries on the kitchen

stove is likely to condense on an upstairs windowpane within a matter of minutes. In the properly designed house this is not to be tolerated. Such a condition is dirty and it is wasteful. The householder should have the power to control the climate produced inside the rooms of his house.

The concern of this chapter is with the creation of the best possible physical environment within the house. Heating takes care of the elementary problem of keeping warm. It stops short, however, of what is technically feasible at the present time and will probably be universal practice in the near future. As good a place as can be found for an approach to this question of climate is the kitchen. Of all the rooms in the house it is the worst offender in producing unpleasant climate. And it is the worst offender because of two essential pieces of equipment—the range and the refrigerator. What the range does has already been described. The role of the refrigerator is probably less familiar.

A refrigerator makes things cold by extracting heat from them. The heat has to go some place, and generally it goes right into the kitchen. During the summer this is particularly objectionable.

A clear course of action is indicated for whoever is planning the kitchen in terms of climate as well as mechanical efficiency. There should be a hood, or at least some kind of collecting duct, over both stove and refrigerator to get the dirt and the unwanted heat out of the kitchen as quickly and as directly as possible.

Hotels and restaurants have been doing this for years by the use of exhaust fans. For the home there is an additional refinement that should be considered. If the exhaust fan were hooked up to a thermostatic control located in the duct or hood, the fan would go on automatically whenever the refrigerator exhaust or cooking raised the temperature a few degrees. This isn't suggested because of a feeling that the housewife is getting soft and is unable even to push buttons any more, but simply because people do forget things, and the remembering might just as well be left to an automatic gadget.

The next offender in order of importance is the bathroom. One advantage of the inside bathroom, already noted, is that it has year-round ventilation, which is more than can be said for the average outside bathroom. People hesitate, quite understandably, to open bathroom windows in cold weather, because the room is used intermittently all day and evening, and, once chilled, takes time to warm up again. A practical way to get around this situation is to install some kind of artificial ventilation and leave the window closed. Some architects have gone so far as to install sheets of fixed glass, thus relying on the window only for light, and an exhaust fan to provide for a change of air. If by any chance the bathroom is located next to the kitchen, possibly the kitchen fan could be made to do double duty.

If we stop and consider the climate question for a moment, we find that we now have the beginnings of a rudimentary system of artificial ventilation which is quite independent of the heating plant. This ventilating arrangement—of fixed glass for light and exhaust fan for change of air—applies to

more than the bathroom and kitchen, because once it is in operation, new air has to come from somewhere, and this somewhere has to be the other rooms in the house. Thus a general movement of air is set up all over the house towards these two rooms. This is far better, of course, than having the air come from them.

A device that has been gaining popularity during the past few years is the so-called attic fan. It has been adopted with particular enthusiasm in the Southwest, and also wherever else the summers get uncomfortably hot. One reason for attic fans is that houses are badly designed. The average pitched-roof house has either an attic or an air space. This air space is not vented to the out-of-doors, with the result that in summer the air trapped under the roof gets so hot that the ceilings below it are turned—literally—into radiators. It is a simple matter to design a house so that air under the roof can be vented as it becomes hot. Farmers have been doing this in their barns and chicken-houses for generations. But because the attics in conventional dwellings have been designed as traps for super-heated air, people have to install these fans to get rid of it. This does not mean that the exhaust fan is a useless apparatus but that it has been misused. Its function should not be to cool the attic, but to control the climate of the whole house. Turned on at night, it brings in the cool outside air, and if the air is dry enough, the result is a refreshing breeze. But the fan doesn't have to be located in the attic, although this is a perfectly good place for it. It could be used to push air into the house as well as to pull it out, and where summers are very humid it could be used in conjunction with a dehumidifying system.

Dehumidifiers are fairly simple pieces of equipment that take moisture out of the air. The commonest type uses a material known as silica gel, which is highly moisture-absorbent. If this silica gel is placed in a chamber through which the air supply for the house passes, it will take moisture out of the air until it becomes so saturated that it can't absorb any more. At this point the equipment provides for removal of the saturated material, which is then heated, usually over a gas flame, until all the moisture has been driven off, and it is then re-used. In most installations the setup consists of a slowly revolving drum, so constructed that part absorbs moisture and part gets rid of it—an arrangement which provides continuous service.

A combination of the items mentioned so far—exhaust fans for kitchens and bathrooms, an attic fan, and a dehumidifier if its use should be desirable—would establish a pretty high level of comfort in the average house if it were installed in conjunction with a first-class heating system. The precise manner in which home ventilation would be handled varies not only with the prevailing summer climate but also with the location of the house. If it is in a city or an industrial neighborhood, the attic fan becomes something of a liability, because the air which is pulled in through the windows is laden with dirt, and cleaning becomes more of a problem than it was before. In such cases the fan should probably be installed in the basement, if there is one, or in a ground-floor utility room, and some type of filter should be used to take the soot out of the air before it hits the fan. Incidentally, there is one rule about the fan itself that should be observed. The bigger it is, the quieter it will be in operation, because to move a given quantity of air through the house a big fan will be operated more slowly than a small one. Ventilating fans up to four feet in diameter, and still larger ones, have been installed in houses.

VENTILATION VERSUS COOLING

At this point one might well ask, "Why not shoot the works and add cooling?" At the present moment there are several reasons why this is not as

good an idea as it sounds. For one thing, a ventilating system requires no ducts; and by the simple expedient of leaving doors and windows open or closed, the flow of air can be directed as desired. With a cooling system, this is not quite as feasible. Ducts are needed, and large ones—a fact that immediately complicates and raises the cost of installation. Added to this is the fact that residential air-cooling is still very definitely in the luxury category. If there is a compressor which requires an electric motor, the motor is generally a big one and costs a lot to run. Another reason is that for houses in most parts of the United States ventilation comes pretty close to doing the job that is needed during the summer months. It is only in the hot and humid central southern regions that air-cooling is desirable in spite of its relatively high cost.

Shortly before the outbreak of World War II, one manufacturer brought out a gas unit designed to handle both heating and cooling in one package. It was fairly expensive, but by no means unreasonably so when compared to any other good installation. The gas flame worked exactly as it does in the gas refrigerator, and tests on actual installations showed that while the cost of summer cooling was fairly high, it was by no means beyond the reach of the middle-class budget. Certainly in the regions where natural gas is cheap and plentiful, units of this type should be highly successful. Possibly with refinements they will become so efficient and inexpensive that they will be suitable for installation in all but the cheapest houses. At the moment, however, this is not the case.

One manufacturer interested in the field of summer air conditioning for houses said that before a cooling system could be sold the owner would have to buy awnings. In the most recent houses where the roof design has been worked out to let the sun in during the winter and keep it out in summer, the awnings would not be required. But the point was well taken. Engineers setting up a cooling system design it with what they call the heat load in mind —that is, they find out how much heat comes into the house, which, in turn, tells them what machinery will be required to get it out again. The smart thing to do, obviously, is not to let it get in, which can be accomplished by proper design, the use of reflective insulation, self-ventilating roofs similar to those installed on barns, and the judicious use of planting.

This last should not be disregarded, because it can be immensely effective. A wall thickly covered with ivy, for example, will never get hot on the inside, no matter how long the sun shines on it, for the green leaves absorb some of the heat and reflect some, while the pattern of the foliage permits a free passage of air currents up the face of the house so that the wall behind never has a chance to get warmed up.

It is conceivable—indeed, quite probable—that all houses will be completely air-conditioned the year round at some future date. At the moment, however, there is not much point in considering it unless there is a generous budget established to cover not only the first cost of the equipment but its use and maintenance as well.

Good climate is something that can be defined rather simply. It involves having clean air at the proper temperature summer and winter, the humidity being kept fairly well under control at all times. For the average house in this country a good ventilating system, coupled with a radiant heating installation and the special handling of kitchens and bathrooms already discussed, will come pretty close to providing optimum living conditions. During the next few years, at any rate, that extra equipment which would provide scientific *perfection* of interior climate will cost more than most of us are willing to pay.

CHAPTER ELEVEN

SLEEPING

OF ALL THE rooms in the house the bedroom has changed least. It would almost be accurate to say that the only essential difference between the sleeping chamber of today and one of the post-Civil War period is the absence of the chamber pot. Because of the simplicity of the activities involved, there has been little incentive to change the equipment. Beds and mattresses have been improved since the days when people threw a blanket over a pile of straw in a corner. And the modern closet with automatic door switches and special hanging gadgets is easier to use than the antique wooden wardrobe. But beds are still horizontal chunks that take up most of the floor space and have to be made and unmade periodically. Closets, while built in and improved somewhat, still show a strong resemblance to old-fashioned clothes cupboards.

This does not mean that when the bedroom is planned there is nothing to do about it. Tremendous changes are about to take place which will influence most of our sleeping habits; but even without these proposed innovations, some of which verge on the fantastic, there is plenty to be done in bringing the bedroom, as a space, up to the standard of quality displayed by more highly developed sections of the house.

Let us take time out and look at the bedroom, not as a room with some standard furniture in it, but as the area in which a great variety of activities takes place. People read in their bedrooms, they dress there, occasionally eat there, frequently smoke, and sometimes write; they may listen to the radio, and they certainly make love.

In a bedroom there is also the question of sleep, which has been studied very intensively by a number of research institutes, and here proper design can, but usually does not, play an important part. The factors having an effect on sleep are noise, whether from within the room or from outside, light, heat, and air. Most people, we strongly suspect, do not sleep particularly well, and the reason for this conjecture is that all of us seem to be able to recall with extraordinary clarity some occasion when we slept especially well. Such an occasion might have been a night in a cabin in a pine woods, where the temperature and quality of the air were the essential factors. City dwellers react very strongly to their first night in the country because of the absence of familiar noises, of which they become conscious only when the source has been removed.

These factors, the scientists tell us, are exceedingly complex, but for our purposes it should be possible to simplify them. The quieter the room, apparently, the more peacefully one sleeps. This has a bearing on design, because rooms can be made quiet. Maximum physical comfort seems to exist when the body is warm and the air a little on the cool side. Typical disturbances such as streaks of light from the nearest lamppost, a reading light in the adjacent bed, or headlights from passing cars, also tend to interfere with sleep. These, too, can be controlled. Thus we see that there are two approaches to planning a bedroom—one based on the creation of the qualities which induce sound sleep, the other based on the other activities carried on there.

THE BEDROOM
AS AN ACTIVITIES CENTER

Some years ago a book was published in Paris by a Swiss architect named LeCorbusier. LeCorbusier was interested in developing entirely new standards for house design, and in the course of his provocative discussion he came to the subject of the bedroom.

No one could have been more emphatic: there should be only one thing in the bedroom, said he, and that was the bed. The idea of dressing in the same space was completely revolting aesthetically and undesirable hygienically. LeCorbusier's fellow citizens were shocked by his attack on what was universally considered a good arrangement.

Quite recently a woman active in public life described to some of her friends the kind of bedroom she would like to have. Nothing could have been more remote from LeCorbusier's ideal of the monastic sleeping chamber, but it made perfectly good sense none the less. The main feature of this bedroom was to be a remarkable motorized bed. Attached to the bed was a kind of dashboard with about a dozen buttons on it: one operated a writing desk, built into the wall, which would swing into position when wanted; another button worked a carefully designed reading light; a third took care of opening and closing the windows; a fourth operated the blinds; a fifth brought a small refrigerated compartment within reach; and others took care of a radio, record-player, maid, telephone, and so on.

There are few of us who spend this much time in our beds, and there are even fewer who could afford the elaborate sets of motors and controls required. Nevertheless, the example does serve to define clearly the range of design possibilities, which in turn represent varying tastes and living habits.

From the foregoing we see that a bedroom can be a great many things. It can be a second living-room, giving members of the family needed privacy for conversation, reading, or study. Or it can be a sleeping chamber which also includes dressing facilities. And, finally, it can be nothing more than a sleeping compartment containing only the beds and the necessary controls for ventilation, light, sound, and the rest.

Fortunately, there is nobody who can tell you which of these kinds of rooms is the best kind. When a house is planned, a choice will be made only on the basis of how one prefers to live. Even this preference, however, will not be completely free, because the budget at some point will enter the picture. Space in a house is comparatively cheap to build—that is, empty space costs less than subdivided space. This means that if a given area is to be divided into a dressing-room and a sleeping chamber, it will cost more than a single room in which both activities are taken care of. Nevertheless, space does cost something, and the bed-living room, which has to be large, will be more expensive than the old-style bed-dressing room.

The sleeping-compartment with separate dressing-room scheme, for example, has one tremendous advantage: the dressing space can be kept warm even if the windows in the sleeping unit are left open all night. There is also the matter of quiet, since a space containing only one or two beds can be very satisfactorily soundproofed at no great expense. The bed-living room scheme, on the other hand, offers the pleasant prospect of sleeping in a room of really generous size with the possibility of a very agreeable, casual kind of existence where one can work or talk without the inconvenience of getting up and going downstairs. Once the choice is made, then it is possible to be very precise.

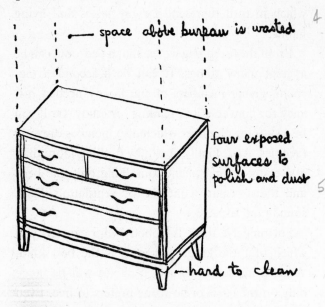

space above bureau is wasted

four exposed surfaces to polish and dust

hard to clean

THROW OUT THE FURNITURE

The bureau is one of the silliest storage compartments ever created by man. It contains three to five drawers, which are twice as wide and as deep as they need be. The bottom drawer is close to the floor, and one generally has to squat to open it. A bureau has four surfaces which are exposed to the room, which means that they must be dusted or polished periodically. It juts out into the room, wasting not only the space where it stands, but a considerable area around it. And it is expensive. The same goes for the taller chest of drawers, normally labeled the chiffonier. These two cumbersome boxes, incidentally, are pushed fairly close to the wall, but since few houses have flush baseboards, they can't be tight against the wall and therefore sit away from it two or three inches. Thus, whenever a collar button rolls off the bureau top, it inevitably rolls between the bureau and the baseboard. Since the chest is hard to move, the space behind it rarely gets cleaned. This inconvenience and waste of time and space is entirely unnecessary. More and more people are discovering

that chests of drawers can be built into a bedroom wall just as the closet is built in.

The dressing table is again a matter of taste. Some women like to use it, others don't. A carpenter can build a shelf with one or two drawers in it, and built-in lighting can be added—all for less than the cost of the spindly-legged jobs currently being merchandised by the department stores. The result can be inconspicuous and attractive, and a lot easier to clean under.

A safe rule to follow, therefore, in planning a bedroom, is to build-in every piece of furniture that can possibly be handled in this manner. The result will be infinitely more satisfactory, unless you happen to be one of those people who feels uncomfortable in a room that isn't stuffed with gimcracks.

PLANNING FOR LIGHT

The bedroom is unique among all the spaces in the house in that it has to be designed both to get light in and to keep it out. Getting light in is simple. It is merely a matter of installing enough windows to let in the daylight and providing enough fixtures to take care of light by night. Fixtures, incidentally, do not mean that funny little gadget in the center of the ceiling which has sockets for three frosted bulbs. It means light in the closets, light on the bed back for reading, light at the dressing table if there is one, and a moderate amount of general illumination, provided by a ceiling cove, a wall fixture, or table lamp. For the child's room, or where one person goes to bed much later than the other, it would be well to take a leaf out of the book of the hospital planners who have long made it a practice to install in patients' rooms small but highly effective shielded lamps which are built flush with the wall at a distance of about eighteen inches from the floor.

Incidentally, getting a decent reading light is by no means a matter of setting a table lamp on the

116

night table. A table lamp would illuminate the whole room, which is awkward in case one person wants to stay up and read while the other wants to sleep; and the lampshade would cut out the light where it is most needed. In recent years any number of fixtures of the spotlight type have been brought out, some specifically for this purpose and others for show-window display. They have the advantage of concentrating all of the light from a low-wattage bulb in a small area so that very little light spills into the room.

plug-in type-night light

built-in type of night light Usually installed a few inches above baseboard.

Keeping the light out of a bedroom is partly a question of personal sleeping habits, partly a question of technique. Some people like to be awakened by the light coming into the room in the morning; others do not. None of us relish the disturbances produced by street lamps and car headlights. Solutions range all the way from light-tight shades equipped with baffles to provide a blackout in reverse, to Venetian blinds, which leak a great deal of light but keep direct rays out of the room.

One trouble with any of the ways of darkening the bedroom is that shutting out the light means keeping out the air as well. All common types of windows share this disadvantage. However, if the window is treated as a fixed piece of glass, with ventilation provided through louvers at the sides

or bottom, it is possible to keep out the light without affecting the flow of incoming air. The window-plus-louver design has been tried by architects in a variety of climates, and it seems to work well. In the chapter on windows it is described in much greater detail, but it should be pointed out here that nowhere are its advantages more apparent than in the sleeping chamber.

CLIMATE FOR SLEEPING

In the final chapter, which attempts to project the most advanced trends in design, some of the really radical proposals for the design of sleeping-rooms are discussed. Here, however, the question is one of solutions that are easy on the average budget. Most of us like to sleep in cool air under warm blankets. In the summertime this can only be achieved by shutting the windows and turning on a mechanical cooling unit. In the wintertime it is somewhat easier, but most of us find that leaving the window open all night makes the air too cold for comfort. Whether cooling is installed in the house or not, mechanical ventilation is probably a pretty good idea the year round. Shutting the windows keeps out whatever noise there is, which is a good idea, and a room thermostat connected to a fan which works on a duct to the bedroom can control the amount of sub-zero air that is admitted in midwinter.

The so-called "room air-conditioner" is a unit which has achieved considerable popularity in hotels, apartments, and individual homes because it is easy to install in existing buildings. If in the days to come these units are reduced in price and made quieter and less conspicuous, they should be worth considering in the sleeping-room, where the door can be shut so that no exchange of air with other parts of the house takes place. Like the fan attached to the duct, they offer the opportunity of getting good air at the right temperature while shutting out whatever outside noises there may be.

117

SLEEPING

THE MULTI-PURPOSE SLEEPING-ROOM

Few houses built these days have enough rooms, because few people can afford to build enough rooms. Moreover, those who can don't seem to want to, because it is so difficult to get servants to take care of them. As a result, a great many kinds of multiple-purpose rooms have come into existence, and most of them involve sleeping as one of the uses. The different arrangements are worth reviewing, because many of them make good sense.

Most common of these two- or three-purpose rooms is probably the library-guest room, which contains a daybed, a comfortable couch, or a bed of the type that fits into a closet. Families who have such a room have long since discovered its usefulness. It can be used as an extra living-room, an emergency sleeping space, or a sick room (this arrangement eliminates running up and down stairs for whoever is caring for the house at the time). From planning small, efficiency apartments, house planners have learned how to convert the living-room itself into a part-time sleeping space. A few families have solved the problem of a nursery by installing folding or sliding partitions between children's rooms so that they can be merged during the day into a single play area. The use of bunks, while inconvenient as a steady diet for adults, is apparently a great favorite with children. Bunks release some bedroom space for other purposes, and occasionally an ingenious architect or parent will have the local carpenter construct a simplified version of the Pullman upper berth which can be folded out of the way when not in use.

WHERE DO THE BEDROOMS GO?

The old and established practice was to put bedrooms all together upstairs. When space got tight and the multiple-purpose room was created, one bedroom moved downstairs. With the trend toward one-story houses all the bedrooms move downstairs. The major planning problem right now is how these rooms should be grouped.

If there is a room or series of rooms for domestic help, a considerable degree of separation should be provided, for the sake of the family as well as that of the servant or servants. If you can afford a guest room it is far better to put it by itself than to merge it with the family bedrooms. Most parents would add to this list of separate sleeping groups the suggestion that the children's rooms also be put off by themselves. Unless there is a nurse around, however, this scheme is impractical while the children are very young.

Certainly the contemporary house is far more livable if the plan takes into account the question of separation. And it is worth taking into account, since bedroom space has to be built somewhere. However, if planning the bedrooms in separate groups involves the installation of an extra bath, it must be remembered that the budget is affected.

This much should be clear from the rather fragmentary discussion above: provision of really satisfactory sleeping space is by no means the cut-and-dried business most of us have taken it to be. Taking a space about twelve by fifteen feet, larger or smaller, installing a closet or two, a central ceiling light, and a long wall, is the traditional way out, and a very easy one, too. More prejudice probably surrounds the whole question of bedroom planning and design than any other section of the house. This prejudice need not necessarily be discarded, but should be examined as dispassionately as possible. A third of our lives is spent in bed, but you would never know it from looking at the rooms most people sleep in.

BEDROOMS AND CLOSETS

116

Whether you choose to make your bedrooms junior
living rooms for private relaxation or to confine
their function solely to sleeping and dressing, there
is no reason why they cannot be as attractive as any
room in the house. The room above, which doubles
as a study and sitting room in the daytime, has been
given a fine window wall opening on a balcony and
overlooking the principal view. The one at the
right, intended only for night-time use, is about as
minimal as a sleeping room for two can possibly be.
Both, however, have been designed with great care
and attention to detail, and each uses modern materials to produce a clean cut, restful effect that is
extremely satisfying.

117

118

119

120

121

An ancient and honorable way to provide for beds is to place them in an alcove (Thomas Jefferson, one of the first modern architects, kept his in one which served as a passage between two rooms, and pulled it up to the ceiling during the day). Views 117 and 118 show two up-to-the-minute versions of the alcove scheme, which is applicable either to the bed-sitting room or—when space limitations are especially stringent—to other rooms as well, to provide accommodation for guests. The pictures above show what architect-designed built-in equipment can do to solve the problem of clothes storage, save floor space, and improve appearance. In view 120, note particularly the handy wall recess for shoes just inside the sliding doors. Such a recess, placed between the partition studs, takes no space at all, and can be built by any carpenter.

124

123

The bedroom above is the handsomest we have come across in a good many years of looking at modern houses all over the country. It is interesting how "at home" in this thoroughly modern room is the bow-back Windsor chair, the best piece of furniture America has produced. For certain functional needs like the dressing table in view 122, the desk in view 123 and the bedback in view 125, modern furniture is mandatory. But do not hesitate to mix in traditional pieces if you happen to feel like it, or insist that the furniture be modern because the architecture is.

127

126

127

134

128

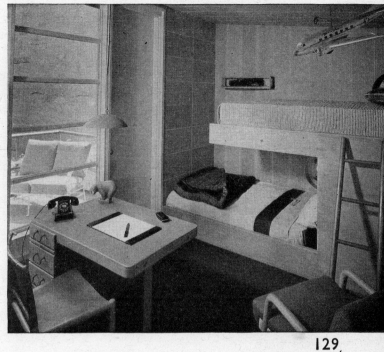

129

130

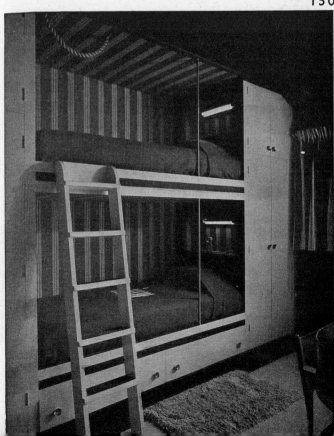

In the sleeping as well as the living portions of the house modern planning ideas can be employed to save space, increase comfort or add entirely new functions to commonplace rooms. View 126, for example, shows how a sliding partition can be used to create a combination bedroom-playroom for the children, sunny and spacious by day, cozy and intimate by night. In the room shown in 127, the same device is employed to divide sleeping and dressing areas, so that the latter can be kept warm all night long. The pictures on this page show several versions of the popular double bunk, including one (129) in which the upper bunk is offset to take advantage of the space above the sloping ceiling of a stairway.

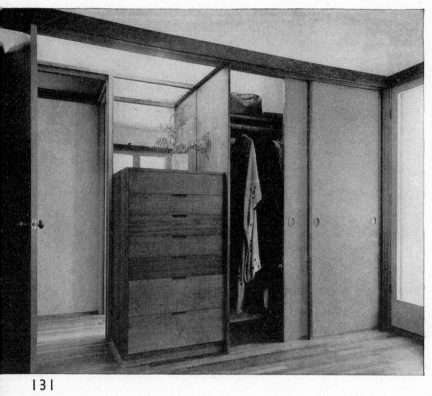

131

132

133

134

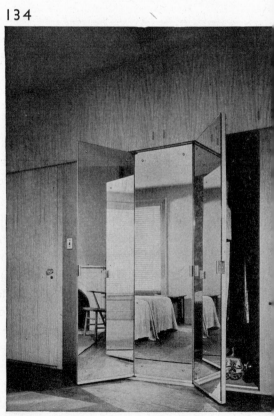

135

Nowhere in the house are the fittings so important as in the bedroom, where space is usually at a premium and the storage question is critical. In the solution of this problem there is almost no limit to what ingenious design can accomplish. A few examples of such ingenuity are shown here: a variety of built-in, space saving chests of drawers; closet doors which also function as a fitting-mirror (134); a minimal guest room (135 and 136) scarcely larger than a good sized bath, but providing a writing desk and fireplace as well as a generous closet. All are carried out in an attractive, economical fashion; the main investment is in design, not in space or materials.

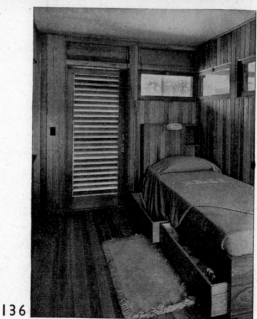

136

137

138

139

140

One criticism frequently leveled at the large windows employed in modern architecture is that they do not leave enough wall space for furniture. The rooms shown here provide a striking refutation of this argument. As view 140 shows, window and furniture design can be integrated in a way that provides a maximum of both glass and storage space, and a simpler, better looking wall to boot. The same principle has been applied to the windows in 139 and 141, while view 138 shows how it can be extended to the bedroom corridor. View 137 shows a storage space for fireplace logs tucked into the bottom of an inside "storagewall" flanking a somewhat similar passage.

141

142

145

143

144

146

147

Built-in storage equipment can make as great a contribution to the living rooms as it does to the bedrooms of the modern house, and it also has the important job of creating functional divisions in the "open plan." Thus the three storage units on the facing page serve as semi-partitions between a dining room and stairway (142), and living and dining rooms (143 and 144—in the latter, note the convenient slots at the end of the unit for card tables and trays). The views on this page show wall-high cabinets for books, and two of the units, 145 and 146, include built-in radio-phonographs. The shelving in 147 is covered by a horizontally-sliding version of the roller desktop.

From storage cabinets and furniture attached to the walls, as in 148 and 149, it is only a step to the use of such equipment to form the walls themselves—a device which we have named the "storagewall." This arrangement takes only a little more space than the ordinary partition, and is extremely flexible, since the various units used to make up a particular wall can be arranged in any desirable pattern and faced in either direction, serving two rooms with the same wall. The wall shown in 150 (which we designed for LIFE) is intended for use between a living room and entrance hall, and is 12 inches thick.

Back of dead storage units opening on hall side

Typical book shelf

148

Back of game closet opening on hall side.

Back of sports and "wet closet".

149

Built-in radio cabinet
Speaker at correct height

Drawer unit houses
record player

Record storage

Built-in desk

Miscellaneous storage

Magazine shelves

Cabinet for vases, etc.

CHAPTER TWELVE

ORGANIZED STORAGE

ONCE UPON A TIME all houses had attics and basements. The basements were full of furnaces, vegetables, garden tools, rubber boots, canned goods, trunks—the familiar combination of junk and useful things a family accumulates. The same was true of attics, except that their contents were mostly junk. World War I had the highly desirable effect of removing a lot of scrap iron from these attics, thus bringing a semblance of order to the storage spaces of millions of American homes. By the time World War II came around, the attics and basements were just as full as they had ever been.

One of the minor miracles in everyone's experience is the annual cleaning bee, during which mother or the entire family, on an appointed day in the spring, swoop up into the attic for the yearly cleaning. The amazing part of this operation is not the elimination of things, but the fact that once the junk is stacked in orderly piles there suddenly seems to be a tremendous amount of space left over, although at the beginning the entire room was so cluttered that you could hardly walk around in it. It is the moral behind this recurring experience that forms the basis for the theme of this chapter; that is, if you have an adequate number of storage spaces, properly shaped and properly located, you can take care of everything that has to be kept out of sight and still have a good deal of space left over.

THE SHRINKING HOUSE

It is common knowledge that the house today is smaller than it used to be. Part of this shrinkage has taken place in the rooms themselves. However, not only are individual rooms smaller, but there are fewer of them. Part and parcel of this process of shrinkage is the gradual disappearance of both attics and basements. Attics have disappeared for a number of reasons. One is the popular practice of tucking bedrooms under the eaves and using dormers to let in the light. Another is the increasing popularity of low-pitched roofs, which do not have a space under them big enough to be used as an attic.

Basements are disappearing for a number of equally good reasons. One is the fact that modern heating plants are compact. The hot air furnaces of thirty years ago, looking for all the world like giant metallic spiders of some antediluvian period, needed plenty of space in the cellar. Since then there has been a shift from coal to oil or gas, neither of which requires cellar space. It is possible that our oil supply may dwindle to the point where it will become less available for heating than it has been; but electricity, which is the most convenient of all, is coming along to take its place. The change in heating equipment, however, is by no means the only reason that basements have shrunk. We don't keep vegetables in them the way we used to, and

135

home canning, at least until World War II broke out, was rapidly becoming a lost art. Finally, the appearance of radiant floor heating may very well eliminate basements, or at least reduce them in the future to tiny storage chambers.

"EQUIVALENT SPACE"

One of the most disagreeable things about small houses built in recent years is that, while basements and attics have shrunk almost to the vanishing point, the builders have included no more space in the general living area. The result for hundreds of thousands of families has been sheer frustration, because in these houses there is no space for trunks, old furniture, or any of the innumerable bulky objects which must be kept around the house. Obviously this is an intolerable situation. The accommodations once provided by cellar and attic must be replaced by equivalent storage space elsewhere. For years the major complaint of the American housewife has been that never has she lived in a house with enough closets. When she says she does not have enough closets, she thinks she means closets; actually she means something quite different. A closet is a place where clothes and blankets and very few other items should be stored. For everything else in or around the house, the closet is no solution at all.

A TIP FROM THE STOREKEEPER

Next time you go down to the corner drugstore, grocery, or delicatessen, look to see how your local merchant stores his wares. There are bins, cupboards, and show cases, but most of the storage is wall storage. A shop-keeper may stock hundreds of individual items, yet he can find any of them in an instant. If he had to sell his stock out of closets, he would go crazy. So would the housewife. In a minor way this is what the housewife is trying to do in the average house.

Just a few days ago, one of us went down to the local hardware store and talked to the owner. How many items did he have in his store? "Well," he said, rubbing his chin, "I don't know. I have never looked at my inventory that way, but I would guess that if you counted everything it would be between six and eight thousand items." Checking over this impressive array of stock we made another discovery: aside from a few very bulky pieces, like wheelbarrows and baskets, garden tools and rope, everything fitted very comfortably on shelves not more than ten inches wide. Let us keep this fact in mind, because it is of the greatest importance in working out a really efficient storage scheme.

BULKY THINGS

Closets are no good for little things because too much space is wasted. They are equally unsuitable for the larger objects which have to be put away in every household. A list of such things would include the baby carriage and, when the children grow older, their bicycles. It would include the lawn mower and the roller, the rakes and luggage, the summer rugs and out-door furniture. Where do they go? In many houses, if there is a basement, they go in the basement. But the chances are that your new house may not have a basement. Certainly no one is going to build a cellar, which is an expensive construction, just for the baby carriage, because it should never get off the ground level, anyway. The same is true of garden tools and bicycles.

One excellent solution for this storage problem is the garage, where there is room to store skis, luggage, summer furniture, and other awkward-to-handle items which are moved only once or twice a year. Some garages are equipped with a kind of storage mezzanine under which the hood of the car will fit, so that still more space is provided. What we are considering here, though, is the question of

136

"Once upon a time all houses had attics...."

possibly making the garage three or four feet wider than it would have to be if only the car were to be considered. This extra footage could be fitted with compartments for the carriage, lawn mower and roller, bicycles, etc., all of which could be taken out and put back easily.

The problem of bulky objects can also be solved independently of the garage. A room for this purpose can be attached to the house, or it can be a kind of super garden shed somewhere out in the yard. If this sounds a little like a return to grandfather's woodshed, what of it? Grandfather had some pretty good ideas.

THE HEATER

If elimination of the basement as a storage space can be compensated for in one of the ways mentioned, or perhaps in some other, we still have to remove the furnace. Can a furnace be placed above ground? In the older types of heating systems which used gravity to get cold air or cold water back to the furnace for reheating, the basement was the only suitable place because it had to be below the level of the lowest living floor. But modern heating systems don't work on gravity, that is, none but the least expensive. The warm air installations, which are generally described as air-conditioning systems, work on a forced draft, using a

blower somewhere in the ducts which pushes the warm air into the rooms and sucks the cold air back in. Reliance on gravity, therefore, is no longer a consideration, and the same is true of the hot-water plants, almost all of which have circulating pumps on the return line from the radiators.

Thus we have the very attractive possibility of putting the furnace or boiler on the first floor, where it can be gotten at easily without any loss of efficiency in heating.

FEW THINGS BELONG IN CLOSETS

Having disposed of the bulky objects, we come to the question of "active storage." Active storage covers everything that is used frequently in the house. It may include a broom, which from this point of view is very active indeed, or a can of stewed tomatoes, which may sit on a shelf for months. They are alike, nevertheless, in that when you want them you want them right away, and without traveling to the other end of the house to get them.

The trouble with ordinary closets when the question of active storage is considered is that they are unorganized space. You can set things in a closet or you can hang them, but there are few things which are satisfactorily taken care of by hanging or leaning.

ORGANIZED STORAGE

Are you one of those unfortunates who has to take a card table out of the front hall coat closet once every week or two? If so, you are familiar with the agonizing process of trying to lift all the coats out of the way and somehow wangling the table out of its hiding place in the back without sweeping all the rubbers and overshoes into the hall. You are lucky if this is all that happens, because in the same closet there may very well be golf clubs, a pair of skis, undoubtedly a set of roller skates, and maybe a couple of umbrellas and a movie projector. Perhaps you keep just a few of these things in your hall closet, but the chances are pretty good that by the time the card table is out you are more in the mood for a stiff drink than a quiet game of bridge.

Here are some of the items that most people, for want of better space, keep in closets: toys, umbrellas, tricycles, hat boxes, luggage, electric light bulbs, overshoes, batteries, wires, tools, tennis rackets, rubbers, movie screens, and sewing machines. Every one of these items, and the dozens you could probably add after going through your own closets, deserves proper storage space, but that storage space should be somewhere else. Moreover, if you get out the tape measure and check the dimensions of these objects, you will find that few of them need a space deeper than ten inches and most would fit in less.

PLACES FOR LITTLE THINGS

We have already seen what shopkeepers, who have to be efficient people, do about storing goods —they use narrow shelves and a lot of them. How does this approach work for the house? We might start with the broom closet in your kitchen, which, if it is one of the standard manufactured units, is a really wonderful thing. Into this cabinet or closet, which is not much more than twelve inches deep or wide, you can put one or two brooms,

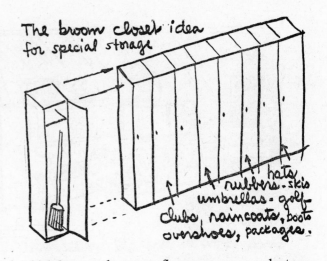

The broom closet idea for special storage

rubbers · skis · umbrellas · golf clubs, raincoats, boots overshoes, packages. hats

whisk broom, dust rags, floor wax, a mop, dustpan, and perhaps a vacuum cleaner. They go in easily and they come out easily. Forgetting the appearance of this unit, let us suppose that the wall in your front hall is ten or twelve inches thick instead of six, so that you have about eight of these broom closets, side by side. A setup like this would give you organized storage space. You could keep your golf clubs, skis, or walking sticks in one; in another, the umbrellas and rain coats. In a third there might be racks for rubbers and overshoes, and so on. The appearance, to be sure, might suggest a typical row of gymnasium lockers, but you would find, if you had an architect worthy of the name, that he could use a very handsome series of wood doors, which would look much better than wallpaper or painted plaster. The joys of a hall so equipped are not yet ended, however, for in the space above the broom closets—or whatever they will be called—there is room for hats, possibly an overnight bag or two—but there is no need to extend this list since you probably have the space filled already. "But what about the card table?" you may ask at this point. "How does one get a card table into a broom closet?" The answer is that you don't, because it is just a matter of making an opening in the end of a wall wide enough for the insertion of card tables, trays, or other objects that have the same general size and shape.

A THEORY OF STORAGE

It should be clear by now what we are driving at. Storage space, if sufficiently specialized, can hold practically anything in the house that has to be put away. As we have already seen, most of these objects are small ones. Now let us look at the house plan. If you take the plan of an average three-bedroom house and put all of the non-bearing partitions (that is, walls which do not serve to hold up ceiling beams) in a straight line, you would probably find that you had about 150 feet of wall in a straight line. This is point one. Now let us assume that this length of wall has been fattened out from 6 inches to 11 or 12 inches so that there is about 10 inches of clear space on the inside. This is point two. Now for point three, which is the payoff: if in these thick walls we installed an average of six shelves, our three-bedroom house would have in its non-bearing partitions a total of 900 running feet of shelf space. Could you use it? We think you could.

This, then, is the theory of essential storage space in the home—the replacement of certain partitions by units which are really cupboards. These partition-cupboards would be scattered through the house according to which rooms make the greatest demands for storage, and they would be made up of open shelves, as in the living-room or library, where we want the books to show; drawers, as in the dining-room or kitchen, where we have to store linens, silver, etc.; or solid doors which look like nothing more than wood paneling, where we want to keep things out of sight.

OBJECTIONS

Realizing that this scheme for storing things might strike practical housekeepers unfavorably, we took the trouble of checking it with a number of people before presenting it here. These were their objections, and perhaps they coincide with some of yours:

1) *Appearance.*—Few like the idea of a wall covered with knobs and handles. As it happens, you can find in some fine old Colonial houses built-in bureaus and cupboards which take up a large part of a wall, and where the knobs and handles on doors and drawers make a very pleasing pattern. Nevertheless, you don't have to have them if you don't want them. There is a kind of spring catch available, to cite one example, where a door is opened by pushing lightly on it. With this kind of hardware, no knobs or pulls are visible. Then, too, drawers can be designed so that they can be pulled out without the use of knobs. Sliding doors can be operated with nothing more than a recessed finger pull. In other words, despite the existence of a great deal of concealed storage space, the walls can be designed so that they give little or no hint of what is going on behind the surface.

2) *Loss of wall space for furnishing.*—When this arrangement was described to one person, she replied that it sounded very well, but what if you wanted to put a table against such a wall? Then the table would have to be moved before you could get to the cupboard. Here the essential flexibility of the storage wall has to be put into play. These storage spaces are accessible, as you choose, from either side of the wall. If the storage wall, were located, let us say, between the living-room and a corridor, the space above table height could open on the living-room side, and the space below could open on the corridor side, and there is a great deal in the way of games and equipment that could be stored in the corridor very appropriately.

3) *Cost.*—Here we have a very real basis for objection. It is not necessary to make elaborate cost estimates to know that this type of wall is going to be much more expensive than a plain partition, but it should be. After all, consider what it can do that a partition cannot. There are very

few places where one can get something for nothing, and a house is definitely not among them. In considering the question of cost, however, there is one mitigating factor that should be considered at this point.

ELIMINATION OF FURNITURE

Let us assume that our first wall-storage unit is going to be installed in the bedroom. In it we will keep the bed linens, possibly extra blankets, certainly all our shoes and hats, perhaps a few books, and, of course, all the clothing now stored in the bureau. With such a wall, we have no need for a bureau or a chiffonier, both of which are normally found in a typical bedroom. And if you felt like getting rid of the dressing table, a pull-down dressing table installed in the wall would work just as well and take up much less space than the kind that stands on legs. By eliminating the bureau, the chiffonier, and possibly the dressing table, a saving can be made in actual dollars and cents. To estimate accurately, however, other factors must also be considered. A great deal of the time spent in cleaning a bedroom is wasted by the necessity of getting underneath various pieces of furniture, dusting and polishing the pieces, and pushing them around. If you hire people to do your cleaning, this saving of labor can be figured in a very precise manner. Should you be one of the majority of people who do their own cleaning, think what the saving of personal wear and tear over a period of twenty years might be worth, again, if you like, in dollars and cents.

Now let us try the dining-room. Here a logical place for the storage wall would be on the kitchen side, because silver, linens, and dishes will be kept in it. With cupboard doors opening front and back, and two-way drawers, we find that the side board and the china cabinet are no longer necessary. If you have really fine dishes, china cabinets are no good for display purposes, anyway. Some section

of the storage wall, fitted with glass sliding doors and illuminated from inside, would turn these formerly hidden heirlooms into a really beautiful wall decoration. Another saving, if you want to try to make it, could be produced by reducing the size of the dining-room somewhat, since at least two bulky pieces of furniture have been eliminated.

In the living-room the same possibilities are evident. The desk could be a hinged unit which would swing out of the wall. If you use a typewriter all the time, a stand for it could be built in. The drawers that make up each side of the conventional kneehole desk are practically useless because things stored in a desk should be kept in very shallow drawers. You will do far better with two dozen one-inch drawers than with the present four- or six-inch drawers; you will be able to store much more and things will be easier to find. The drawers of tables in living-rooms, at least most of the tables whose owners have allowed us to look inside of them, are stuffed with playing cards, photograph albums, ash trays, poker chips, extra cigarettes, old theater programs, etc. If you cannot bear to throw out any of these rarely looked at mementos, you would still be better off if they were stored behind a wall and out of sight.

A short while ago we asked a famous industrial designer what he thought the best radio cabinet was. In a burst of unbusinesslike honesty, he replied, "No cabinet. The best place for a radio and speaker and record-player is in the wall some place so that you don't have to dust it and you don't have to look at it except when you are using it." Following this suggestion, we would therefore be inclined to take our radio out of its fancy imitation Chippendale cabinet and tuck the works into the storage wall. Placing the speakers in one of the upper units would give far better acoustical qualities. To hold the record-player and records, the wall would have to be more than ten inches thick, which suggests that the wall as a whole be made deeper, or certain cabinets in its lower portion be made as wide projecting units. Records and albums and sheet music could all be stored in such cabinets. So could the movie projector and the bulkier kinds of amusement apparatus.

If it is your family's habit to serve cocktails or highballs in the living-room, it is convenient to keep bottles, glasses, and ice bucket in the storage wall. It would be a very simple matter to build the front of this bar unit as a shallow metal-lined tray which, when let down, would provide a safe water-proof surface on which to mix the drinks.

These suggestions, of course, barely touch the possibilities of the storage wall, and uses of the wall would vary widely from one family to another. If family A collects ivory elephants, and family B likes pictures, and family C is proud of its collection of fine books, and family D subscribes to thirty weekly and monthly magazines, these units would be used in totally different ways. Everyone would be completely satisfied, too. The books and the elephants could be displayed most effectively, while the magazines, if installed in slanting racks, would be interesting to look at and easy to find. In other words, what we have here is another instance of standardization functioning not as a straight-jacket but as a means for freeing the ex-

pression of family tastes. The storage wall is just a framework. It becomes what one makes of it.

WHY HAVE CLOSETS?

It would seem from the foregoing that the good old closet has been practically eliminated. Such is almost the case, but not quite. What has been done eliminates closet storage for almost everything except clothes, and now, relieved of the necessity of doing things for which it is totally unfit, the closet can become an extremely efficient special unit. As a shallow box a little less than two and a half feet deep, it becomes a perfect unit for suits and dresses. Actually, a hanger with clothes on it can be accommodated in a still narrower space, but we must provide clearance for the moth bags in which summer and winter clothes will be put.

The design of the efficient clothes closet is simple. The hanging rod should be high enough to accommodate long evening dresses. Everyday clothes hung from this height will be quite convenient to get at, so there is no need to install two sets of bars. This shallow type of closet should have an opening across its entire front. Whether you use sliding panels or swinging doors does not matter, although it has been our experience that the latter are far more convenient. But a full opening must be pro-

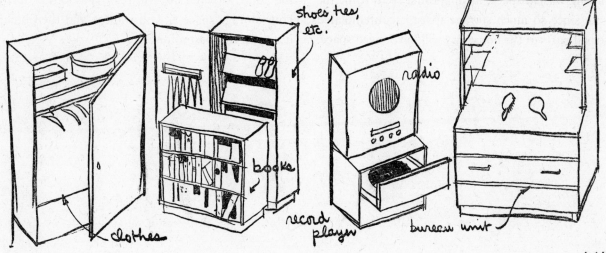

vided in one way or another, because nothing is more annoying than trying to reach in through a narrow door to find clothes at the end of a shallow closet. In this closet there will also be a light over the door. Tube lights extending the full length of the opening inside would be ideal. If the upper part of the space is to be used for blankets and odds and ends, it should have its own door above the door to the closet proper so that they will be easy to get at. The floor should be raised somewhat to keep out dust from the bedroom, and all the corners should be curved for easy cleaning. Cleaning, by the way, will be pretty easy, because shoes and other things that used to clutter up the closet floor will now be installed in one or another of the special wall cabinets. The approach to the storage problem, as we now see, is by no means a matter of installing a lot of closets. It involves a very thoughtful estimate of what you want to keep where, how big it is, and how often it has to be taken out or put back. The solutions will range all the way from an enlarged garage or storage shed out in the back yard to slots in the walls and special cupboards, shelves, and drawers of the most varied types. Once this part of the planning process has been gone through and the right spaces have been provided, the same thing that we discovered when the attic was cleaned will be evident. Instead of having wasted space, as might first seem to be the case since so much storage space is contemplated for all parts of the house, we will have saved space.

We will not be putting handkerchiefs, which require two-inch drawers, into drawers which are six inches deep. Dishes ten inches in diameter will not be stacked in kitchen cupboards which are sixteen inches deep. The house planned on this basis will have more storage than anyone ever dreamed was possible in a dwelling of reasonable size; and yet, because there will be a place for everything and much useless furniture will be eliminated, there will also be more space for unencumbered living.

Don't think that planning this kind of a house is easy. It isn't. But a lot more will come out of the work than went into it, because planning a house is at the most a matter of months and using it can run into generations. It would be wonderful, indeed, if we could go down to the local building-supply house tomorrow and order the storage wall units and the closets we would like to have; but we can't. Nobody makes them yet, although the time is not far off when they will be made. In the meantime it will be necessary to rely on the carpenter and the cabinetmaker, who will have to build these walls from special designs, and the cost will inevitably be higher. Some of this added expense can be made up from savings on furniture and savings in maintenance, but not all of it. As for the difference, you will just have to make up your mind to spend some extra money, because the added expenditure will really pay off. So plan your storage space as you want it and then build it as you can best afford it.

CHAPTER THIRTEEN

SOUND CONDITIONING

ABOUT FOUR years ago we had occasion to make a general survey of what had happened to the design of broadcasting studios. These rooms presented immensely difficult acoustical problems, partly because of the nature of radio broadcasting itself, partly because the rooms must be sufficiently flexible in their engineering design to permit the perfect reproduction of sounds ranging all the way from the voice of one person to the very complex noises made by an entire orchestra. Our assumption when the research was begun was that acoustics as a science had a very precise basis, and that the first broadcasting studios had been calculated with as much efficiency as the most recent. Nothing could have been farther from the truth.

One of the earliest studios examined had been built in 1928. It was a plain rectangular room with sound-absorbing material on the ceiling. It must have been quite unsatisfactory from the acoustical point of view, but at that time so were the receiving sets, and the demand for fidelity was not nearly so great as it became in subsequent years.

Another studio, built in 1932, was still a rectangular room except that the corners had been replaced by diagonal walls, and acoustical material was used not only on the ceiling but also on some of the walls. Six years later the Columbia Broad-

casting System installed some studios the like of which had never been seen in this country. The walls, instead of going straight up and down, were tilted. Strange broken surfaces jutted out into the room. On certain walls where sound-absorbing material had been used, there were panels of plywood designed to reflect sound and to give it resonance. In the most recent of the studios the walls have been shifted around so that they are not parallel to each other, and the ceilings have been broken up so that no section of this surface is parallel to the floor. What this adds up to is that acoustical science, presented with very specific and admittedly difficult problems, has completely altered room design in an interval of barely more than a decade. Today the engineers are sufficiently well equipped in knowledge and experience to help the architect produce any kind of acoustical effect in any kind of interior.

Possibly you have never thought of acoustical design in connection with your home. Nevertheless, sound control can be a vital factor in improving livability and establishing a greater degree of privacy. Moreover, the smaller the house, the greater the need to pay attention to this completely neglected factor in house design. It is possible—and, we feel, highly probable—that at some point in the future the rectangular shapes now considered standard for rooms will be abandoned in favor of other shapes which to any of us at the moment would look very strange.

Some of these shapes will be brought into existence by the requirements of large-scale factory production, just as your car over a period of forty years has changed from an assembly of flat planes and sharp corners to the present complex machine whose every surface is part of a compound curve. This belongs to the future, however. The purpose of this chapter is to examine what can be done with the house as it is being designed today and will continue to be designed in the forseeable tomorrow.

ACOUSTICS IS A NEW SCIENCE

The broadcasting studios, as we have seen, were the first building interiors to react sharply to the demands for higher fidelity of sound reproduction. This is as it should be, for while a very few people can see what is going on in a broadcasting studio, tens of millions can hear. When sound came to the movies, theater design changed. The good movie houses of the late thirties and early forties showed the effect of talking pictures very clearly. Again we find two characteristics: one is the abandonment of parallel walls or surfaces; the other is the use of carefully designed surfaces, some of which reflect sound very brilliantly while others absorb it almost completely.

Next to feel the effect were the offices, particularly those large rooms where thirty to three hundred typewriters might be clacking away at the same time. In these spaces it was found that acoustical plaster on the ceiling or those attractively textured and perforated tiles did a great deal to reduce the general noise level. This was done not merely to increase the well-being of the employees—although it did have that effect—but because the experts who carefully studied the causes of fatigue and its relation to output found that greater effi-

ciency paid for such installations in a very short time.

It was also found that sound could be controlled to an appreciable extent by the use of noiseless typewriters, which brings up a third procedure that can be applied to the design of the house—the elimination of noise at its source.

The next building type to fall in line was the factory. When the war broke out and billions of dollars were invested in the construction of new industrial plants, it was found that what held for office workers and their morale and efficiency was also true for factory workers. We have already described the immense bomber plant in the Southwest whose mile-long walls and ceiling are packed full of sound-absorbing material. This was not as expensive as it may sound, because the acoustical material is also used for insulation against heat and cold. This is another expedient that the home builder may consider: multiple use of materials so that the expense for any given requirement is not too great.

ACOUSTICS IN THE HOME

We now have four techniques with which to attack the problem of sound control in the home. The question is, what is this problem we are trying to attack? For the average family it breaks down into two parts. The first is the matter of maintaining complete quiet in certain areas—let us say, in the bedroom where a small child is sleeping. A solution of this would be letting the child sleep without forcing the rest of the family to go about on tiptoe.

The second general situation is one where conflicting activities—acoustically speaking, of course—are carried on in the same room or in the same part of the house. For example, father wants to read the paper, mother wants to carry on a long telephone conversation with a friend, and the children want to listen to the latest installment of some radio thriller. The resulting acoustical conflict is normally left unsolved, except in the houses of the very rich where there is enough space for the various members of the family to get away from each other.

In addition to these two very common situations there frequently arises a third. That is, when the family takes great pleasure in listening to the radio, to phonograph records, or to music produced by the family itself. If you take a five hundred dollar radio with all of the wonderful quality which has been built into it and put it into the average small living-room, the chances are that it will not sound much better than a fifty dollar radio. However, we are told by the acoustical engineers that a living-room can be designed so that its sound characteristics are not very different from those of a full-scale symphony hall; that it is possible, in other words, to design this room so that your five hundred dollar radio (or even the fifty dollar one, for that matter) gives a performance comparable in quality to that of an orchestra.

Those who are interested in obtaining this special added livability for their home must use an architect who is willing and able to work with a first-rate acoustical engineer as a consultant. We say "willing" because the room that will result from a successful collaboration on the part of these two technicians will be rather unconventional though far from unpleasing in shape, and it certainly will not fit comfortably into any known kind of "period" house.

One of us had occasion recently to design a house in New York where a major factor in the design of the living-room was precisely this acoustical quality. The best radio-phonograph combination obtainable was not considered good enough, and one was specially built. Also, there were two pianos. By the time the architects and engineers got through, one wall was padded to a depth of several inches with rock wool and covered with a kind of grass matting which allowed the sound to go through the surface; the other wall was paneled

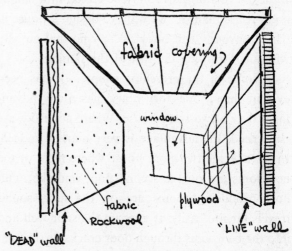

with sheets of oak plywood held loosely in place so that the proper brilliance of sound could be obtained; the two end walls, which were entirely of glass, were set so that they were not parallel to each other. The ceiling was constructed of wood frames covered with stretched linen, and behind the linen were some areas filled with broken sheets of wallboards so that sounds would be reflected in an irregular manner; other parts of the ceiling were heavily padded with rock wool.

This was admittedly an extreme procedure, and it was by no means cheap. The results, however, were extraordinary as far as quality of sound is concerned, and the room's appearance generally produced a favorable impression. The only point of this example is that while such a procedure does not apply to the house of minimum cost, it most definitely is not restricted to houses for the very rich. Just as in the bomber plant, the rock wool padding on wall and ceiling can be used for heat insulation as well as sound absorption. And finishing materials such as linen and grass matting are by no means beyond the reach of the middle-class budget.

However, let us return to the more general questions of how to establish quiet zones within the house and how to reduce the discomfort produced by conflicting family activities.

SOUND CONDITIONING

OBJECTIVE OF SOUND CONDITIONING

Basically this objective may be stated in a simple and precise manner: we want to design a house in which anybody can carry on any normal activity without disturbing the rest of the family.

In some of the preceding chapters it has been evident that a one-story house has many advantages over a two-story house. Where acoustics are concerned, the advantage is very marked indeed. In the average two-story house where most of the bedrooms are on the second floor and the main noise-producing rooms are on the first, sound travels far too easily. It goes up the stair well and into the bedrooms through door cracks or through the doors themselves. It also goes through the floor boards, which function in much the same manner as a drum—that is, any sounds picked up by one surface are given off by the other. Two-story houses have their advantages. Their compactness is perhaps the greatest. But, acoustically speaking, they have no merit whatsoever.

It is possible—and, for that matter, it has been done—to build multi-storied houses whose acoustical properties are admirable. But this generally involves the elimination of wood construction in favor of some heavy type of fireproof building where the second floor is of reinforced concrete or an equally dense and weighty material. Few people, however, can afford to pay for this kind of construction, and many of those who can feel that it is pretty much a waste of money. If an attempt is made to achieve the soundproof qualities of the concrete-and-masonry house while using wood, something could possibly be worked out in the way of separating floor and ceiling construction. But it would be costly and not very effective.

Turning to the one-story house we find the following advantages: A one-story house of necessity places its bedrooms at some distance from the main living areas, and distance alone is a factor in sound control. The bedroom corridor, unlike the stair well, can be treated very easily so that sounds which do penetrate into it are absorbed and stopped. It is also possible to put sound barriers between the noisy rooms and the quiet rooms. Among those that might be considered, a stone wall with a fireplace in it comes close to being ideal, because, as a rule, the thicker and heavier the barrier, the less likelihood there is of penetration by sound. If there is no fireplace, a thinner wall of cinder block or some such material is very effective. A bank of closets is also a satisfactory sound-stopper, should the plan permit such an arrangement.

The essential advantage, however, is the factor of separation, with the possibility of stopping the sound before it gets too close to the rooms from which it should be excluded.

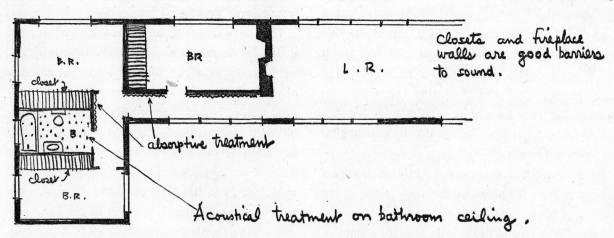

Closets and fireplace walls are good barriers to sound.

absorptive treatment

Acoustical treatment on bathroom ceiling.

PREVENTION OF NOISE AT THE SOURCE

Anything done to stop sound where it originates works exactly like the traditional ounce of prevention—it eliminates the need for a cure. Let us consider some of the rooms that are the worst offenders.

These rooms include the living-room, dining-room, kitchen, playroom, and bathroom; of these, the bathroom is the most annoying because it can be the most embarrassing. Everyone is familiar with the disagreeable interruption made by the noisy flushing of a toilet adjoining the main living space. And it is an unfortunate coincidence that the water closet, for functional reasons, is shaped almost like a trumpet. A trumpet, as one might well imagine, is no shape for suppressing noise at its source. Conceivably something could be done to modify the design of the present-day water closet to produce a shape more satisfactory acoustically and equally efficient in other respects. However, since no such water closet exists, we may as well forget it for the time being.

Because of this unfortunate design we have a clearly unhappy situation, and one which is heightened by the fact that the ideal bathroom, as seen by most prospective homeowners, is an interior in which all the surfaces are hard, waterproof, and therefore highly sound-reflective. Here is where we find the opening wedge for our attack on bathroom noises at their source. In the first place, soil lines—that is, the pipes which carry waste matter from the bathroom fixtures—can be packed in insulating material, which tends to deaden noise somewhat. Tile and hard plaster can be replaced by such materials as sheet rubber, linoleum, and other materials which are water-repellent and also resilient. This helps to reduce reflected noise. On the ceiling a standard acoustical material can be used—either one of the plasters manufactured specifically for this purpose, or the perforated metal panels, or perforated or textured fiber boards which have been on the market for some years.

The floor can be covered with a soft rather than a hard material. The upper parts of the walls, that are not exposed to moisture can have the perforated acoustical materials already mentioned. In addition, a heavy flush door, weather-stripped in the bargain, would do a great deal to reduce the direct transmission of sound. This weather-stripping, incidentally, need not consist of anything more than a strip of felt, rubber, or some other material permitting a tight seal to be made, and it would be attached to the door stop.

Location of the bath can be as important as any of these suggested control measures. For example, if we are considering a downstairs lavatory, it could be arranged to reduce transmission of sound. In one such arrangement there is a fireplace wall between it and the living-room, and the coat closet off the front hall serves as an entry. Remember, by the way, that a closet is a wonderful sound barrier, because the clothes will absorb any sound that passes through.

This combination closet-sound barrier also suggests an excellent solution for the telephone problem, because if a little telephone desk is incorporated with the closet-corridor, conversations can be carried on without annoying anyone who might be trying to read or study in the adjoining living-room.

Acoustical control, it must be emphasized again and again, is as much a matter of thoughtful planning as of installation of special materials. It is true that under certain conditions planning won't do the job, and special materials have to be used. A good example of this is the open-front telephone booth used in New York City's newest subway. There, even with the terrific clatter of passing trains, it is possible to carry on an intelligible conversation. This seeming miracle is the result of using three walls of sound-absorbing materials for the booth.

In the house where the corridor-closet-phone room combination isn't possible, some variation of this scheme would work very well, for it takes up very little space and costs very little money.

THE KITCHEN

The annoyances produced by the hired girl in the kitchen, who tosses your best china around with the utmost abandon while you are trying to be polite to your husband's boss after dinner, are too well known to require extended description. Even if there is no hired girl and no ceremonial dinner, the noise problem remains.

There are some expedients for cutting off the sound at its source, but they are by no means 100 per cent effective. Among them are the replacement of enameled metal surfaces, such as drainboards, with work counters of wood, perhaps covered with linoleum or rubber. A dish or pot dropped on such a surface will land with a dull thud instead of a noisy crash. Rubber-covered wire dish baskets which fit into one's sink if there is a double sink, or into the laundry tray if there is a combination unit, are, again, exceedingly effective in muffling noise. The type of sink which appeared before the war, usable as a dishpan as well as a sink, also can help control sound, because once filled with water the noise of dish and pot washing is materially subdued. Over and above this, there is the possibility of sound barriers or sound traps of one kind or another.

It is a very convenient characteristic of sound that, like light, it does not readily travel around corners. Thus, if you plan a small pantry or utility space between the kitchen and the dining-room or the living-dining room, the wall facing the kitchen door could be covered with sound-absorbing material, and what noise did get beyond this secondary space would be greatly reduced.

In addition to this, however, the home builder should consider an acoustically treated ceiling and a resilient floor for the kitchen. These should be installed not only to keep the noise out of the other rooms but also to make work in the kitchen itself more agreeable. An empty room—and the kitchen is, acoustically speaking, empty—is far less pleasant than a room containing sound-absorbing materials. You can check this for yourself very easily by recalling the difference in sound between a furnished living-room and the same space before the furniture and carpets were moved in. The hollow echoing sounds we associate with uninhabited houses or apartments are the kind we usually get in the inhabited kitchen. It just happens that in the kitchen we are used to them and in living-rooms we are not. Acoustically treated surfaces in the kitchen would perform the same function as upholstered furniture and carpeting in the other rooms. And who is to say that a kitchen, where most of the housewife's time is spent, should be less agreeable in its atmosphere than the living-room?

CONTROL WITHIN ROOMS

The things discussed so far are concerned chiefly with keeping noise in one space from getting into another. What about the family living-room where three separate kinds of noises may be produced within the same space at the same time? Obviously, there is not going to be a perfect solution, because even if it were technically obtainable it would cost too much. Nevertheless, there are some highly desirable expedients. Take the case of the radio, for example.

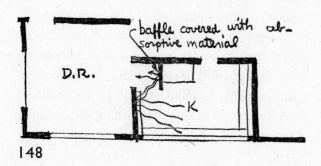

If the radio faces a sound-absorbent wall, there will be two immediate results: the room will seem much larger as far as the sound is concerned; and noise hitting the opposite wall will not be reflected, thus reducing the over-all disturbance.

Now what about the person who wants to sit and read or study while the radio is going? As we have seen, the noise cannot be eliminated, but it can definitely be reduced. And the solution is partly planning, partly use of materials. If the living-room is made an L rather than a rectangle, and the smaller part of the L is used as a library alcove, and if, moreover, the long side of the living-room is covered with sound-absorbing material, noise would not be reflected around the corner. It is pretty likely that this alcove, though completely open to the living-room, would be a remarkably quiet and pleasant place even if a considerable amount of noise were being manufactured in the rest of the room.

If this doesn't prove to be enough, the list of expedients is by no means exhausted. A double-faced row of bookcases projecting out into the room automatically creates a kind of alcove. Books themselves ranged on shelves are an exceedingly effective sound trap. Thus if the noise problem is sufficiently acute, our sound-controlled living-room might consist of a large space subdivided by a baffle and an alcove. In such a room the average family could carry on its separate activities with a privacy undreamed of in the average American home.

This chapter has been anything but a technical treatise on acoustics, yet we have managed to examine the many problems of sound control in the house and some of the techniques developed in other types of buildings. We have learned that sound does not travel easily around corners. We know that getting around them can be made even harder by putting sound-absorbing materials on the reflecting surfaces. We know that baffles acoustically treated as in the open-front telephone booth can produce privacy within a space without breaking up that space. From the office designer we have learned that treatment of the ceiling with sound-absorbing materials and treatment of the floor with resilient materials or even with carpeting can work wonders in reducing the general noise level.

It is evident that planning, if carried out with the question of sound control in mind, can be extremely effective, and that a little ingenuity in such places as the kitchen can turn it into a quiet and agreeable work space.

If you are hesitating for any reason whatever between a one-story plan and a two-story plan, the question of acoustics may help in arriving at a decision, in spite of the obvious fact that nobody who wants a two-story house is going to shift to a plan for a single floor just because some of the rooms might become quieter.

ACOUSTICS AS DECORATION

One reason people have been slow to adopt techniques developed in offices and other types of non-residential interiors is that they have felt that their own home interiors would somehow lose charm in the process. As far as sound control is concerned, there is nothing whatever to worry about. Everybody likes exposed masonry walls whether of stone or brick, and when these are used inside the house —and there are many such examples in the photographs scattered through this book—not only is the wall texture greatly enhanced but sound barriers are automatically set up. In the most modern of modern houses and the most conservative of conventional houses, masonry walls are used with the greatest willingness by architects and their clients alike. Therefore, consider such surfaces not only as acoustical factors but also as a decided advantage when the question of decorating comes up.

Everyone likes wood, too. There has seldom

149

been a house where the owner has not been more than willing to install wood paneling. Ten or fifteen years ago this was rather expensive, because good wood such as mahogany or walnut or oak could only be purchased in solid pieces, and the panels had to be installed by expert craftsmen. Wood paneling, therefore, has always been associated in the popular mind with luxury.

Today this limitation no longer exists. Any of the big plywood companies can furnish laminated sheets four feet by eight feet in size, or larger, veneered with woods so rare and exotic that their use hitherto has been confined to the most expensive furniture. There is little question about the desirability of using such woods in the average living-room or even in the master bedroom. Some people are so fond of flush plywood paneling that they have installed it in their bathrooms. With the new finishes available on the market, these panelings can be made highly water-resistant.

Here we have the chance to combine improved home decoration with ideal sound conditioning.

And remember that the few dollars an acoustical engineer might charge for his consulting services is not going to affect your total budget much one way or another. Get his advice.

Sound control techniques embrace many modern materials in addition to wood and stone. Fortunately, they are all agreeable in appearance and rich in texture. The acoustical plasters are much softer and much better textured than the white plaster that goes on the average ceiling. The same is true of the perforated panels, which can be painted any color and any number of times without impairing in any way their high efficiency as sound absorbers. These, too, work in particularly well with the contemporary decorating scheme, where the attempt is to get textural richness through the use of machine-produced forms rather than the fakery of bygone handicraft techniques.

Thus we can end with the assurance that the sound-conditioned house will not only be pleasanter to live in because it will be quieter, but that it will be much better to look at.

152

153

154

WINDOWS

Big, well designed windows are the trademark of modern architecture. They are the means of bringing together the outdoors and indoors in an integrated visual and functional pattern that makes living in modern houses an exciting new experience. Made possible by modern developments in building technology, they can be used to reduce fuel bills and increase comfort. In one form or another, they are applicable to every building problem, and modern architects seem able to go on discovering such new forms and new applications indefinitely. The examples on this page suggest the range of this experimentation: a two-story dormer for a studio-workshop in Delaware (152), a foldaway window-wall in a living room overlooking a California hillside (153) and an unusual combination of sash, fixed glass and glass block from a suburban house near Philadelphia (154).

Not every house can enjoy the perfect setting of the one above, but when such an opportunity does come along it is one of the virtues of modern design that it is capable of exploiting it to the maximum. And on the ordinary suburban lot, where nature does not provide the view, it is possible to manufacture it, as the other examples shown here demonstrate. Such effects depend on the most intimate sort of collaboration between the designer of the house and the landscape architect, and require more than a nominal investment in spiky evergreens. They pay off, however, in a feeling of spaciousness that can make a compact house seem twice its true size.

The big glass areas and movable walls used in modern houses are not only capable of brightening old types of rooms; they are creating entirely new types. Thus the space above (159) is neither a porch nor an inside room, but a combination of both. View 160 shows a glazed passage that doubles as a porch, view 161 an outdoor living space connected to a bedroom by a sliding door. On the facing page, 162 and 163 show a sunporch that can be completely open or completely enclosed, view 164 a modern version of the old-fashioned "conservatory," with a glazed roof. Connected by sliding doors to a glass-walled living room, this room won the grand prize in a contest for new uses of glass in building construction.

162

163

164

165

166

167

168

169

170

The logical final development of the glazed, sliding wall is the living room that becomes a porch simply by pushing away the wall, and becomes a room again by closing it. This arrangement makes lots of sense, since one set of furniture serves for both outdoor and indoor living, and there is no need to put away chairs and tables in bad weather. The three rooms shown here are all true part-time-porches in which at least one full wall can be removed completely. With present day equipment and weatherstripping, such walls slide easily and can be made virtually draftproof. In winter, they can be opened slightly for ventilation.

171

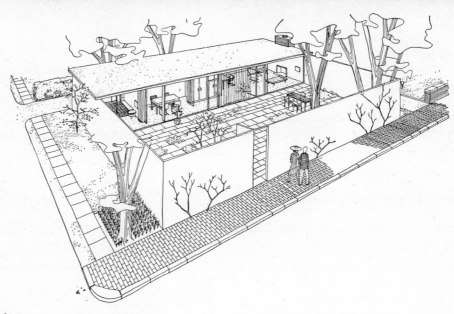

172

173

174

175

An obvious objection to the use of glazed walls in built-up areas is lack of privacy. These designs show how it can be avoided. Two of the houses (171–173 and 172) employ almost identically the same scheme: a continuous glass wall facing a garden enclosed by a high fence; in one case, to permit free passage of air, the fence is built like a venetian blind standing on end. Another solution is the "patio" plan in which the rooms themselves enclose the garden, as in 174. Views 175 and 176 show two more versions of the walled-garden idea, one for a small lot, the other for a large one.

176

178

When an entire wall, or a large part of a wall is made of glass, there is no necessity to use ventilator sash over the whole area. Big pieces of fixed glass are better looking, easier to clean (when on the ground floor), easier to make weathertight, and cost less than a complex assembly of movable windows. One of the simplest and most dramatic schemes is to use floor-to-ceiling panes of plate glass (set in the type of frame used for store windows) over most of the area, supplemented by metal sash, as in 177 and 178. And, where fixed glass is used, there are convincing arguments for using louvres rather than glass in the part of the window given to ventilation, as in 181 and 182.

179

180

181

182

In lighting a large room, a given
high in the walls is twice as eff
amount at or below eye level. In
it is often possible to place such
center of the room, as in 183 a
flood the entire interior with da
tensity. Skylights can also perfor
tion in bringing the lighting in th
the house up to the standard of t
View 187, for example, shows an
in this way. Had this skylight l
corridor might have seemed exc
relation to other parts of the hou

183

188

184

189

190

191

In hot weather, the big windows used in modern architecture would admit entirely too much sunshine if they were not protected in some way. Commonest solution for this problem is the use of "hoods," or permanent sunshades proportioned so as to cut out most of the summer sun while letting in as much as possible in winter—a device which works to perfection on windows facing south. Two such hoods, one used to form a porch, are shown in pictures 188 and 189. An idea of the accuracy with which they operate can be obtained from 190 and 191, which show the outside of one "solar" house in midsummer and the inside of another in midwinter. In the second view, notice how far into the room the low winter sunshine penetrates, bringing heat that cuts fuel bills substantially.

CHAPTER FOURTEEN

WINDOWS

WINDOWS HAVE been in houses almost as long as there have been houses. There have been windows of ice and rock crystal and mica and nothing at all. The most commonplace, the most completely familiar part of a house that there is, the window seemed to most people so simple a thing that generations went by before it occurred to anyone to do any thinking about it. And when they finally began to think, they discovered some very strange and wonderful things.

Did you know that the window out of which you look to see if Johnny is coming home from school, or if the milkman is coming by with that extra quart—that window so clear and perfectly transparent—is really as opaque as a solid slab of armor plate? Did it ever occur to you that this fragile sheet is daily throwing back a bombardment of rays of all sizes and shapes?

It was only when some scientifically minded people began to look at the common pieces of glass we have taken for granted for so long that they found they were dealing with an amazingly complex apparatus, built like a dam with countless billions of tiny sluice gates which unerringly opened and closed to let some things through and to keep others out.

When the scientists got through, a few architects in various countries began piecing together the bits of data, wading through formulas and graphs and other scientific jargon, to find out what this meant in terms of buildings. None of these architects was particularly important or financially successful, and this was probably because their curiosity far outweighed their business acumen. While their fellow professionals were saying in an unconscious parody of Gertrude Stein, "A window is a window is a window," these people were saying "Is it?" and "What is it?" and "Why is it?"

One of the little tidbits they picked up, a typical and apparently unrelated scientific fact, is that glass is opaque to low temperature radiation; that is, while wide open to most of the heat of the sun, it is closed to the infra-red waves sent off by any object cooler than a steam radiator. This is one reason why the greenhouse makes such a good heat trap. It is also the reason why the solar house is possible. But glass, as everyone knows, is also opaque to the bulk of the ultra-violet rays. In other words, the average window is a very narrow gate through which only a little more than visible light can pass. Attempts to widen it have been pretty expensive or not very successful, but location of the gate in the spectrum can be shifted. In terms of the home, what does this mean?

Some years ago a product called Vita Glass was put on the market. It was intended to do everything window glass did and let in ultra-violet as well. This was an attempt to "widen the gate"— to let in a broader slice of the spectrum. It was a good idea. People in homes glazed with Vita Glass would have had fewer germs to contend with and might have gotten a coat of tan in the bargain. But

167

it never got down to a price home builders could afford.

The windows in your car are not made of single sheets of glass, but are a sandwich with a transparent plastic sheet as the filler. The virtue of these windows is that they are shatterproof. It is rarely that a home builder feels the need to go to extra expense for this reason, but we ran across a large house in Pittsburgh a while ago whose playroom windows were equipped in this manner. A far more useful filler is air, whose insulating properties are well known to anyone who has put up a storm sash. The advantage of the "air-glass sandwich" is that it removes the need for the extra sash. Double glass is widely used in modern trains. One such product available for homes is "Thermopane," a sealed package consisting of two thicknesses of glass with a quarter-inch air space. It costs a little more than twice as much as a single sheet of glass, but less than a window plus storm sash. The small air space, by the way, provides quite as good insulation as a much bigger gap would.

WINDOW MECHANICS

Even more important than glass is the kind of window in which it is installed. There are many types, some comparatively new and unfamiliar, others which have been in use for centuries. The type of window selected for a house has to do with much more than operating characteristics and price, for windows, more than any other element in the house, set its "style." Not many of us realize this, but the way we identify houses as Colonial, English, French Provincial, and so on, is pretty much by the window pattern, which is different in each case. Similarly, an outstanding characteristic of the modern house is not a flat roof or some new material, but the radically different manner in which the windows are set.

The double-hung window is common in our country because it is cheap, simple to install, and practically foolproof mechanically, since all it has are pulleys and sash weights (or balances) and a handle. It is also a pretty good ventilator, because it can be opened from the top or bottom or both.

The second important type of window is the casement. Casements trace their ancestry back to the great houses of medieval England. This doesn't mean that the casement was invented in England, but it does relate to a certain type of medieval building, just as the double-hung window is a fundamental design element in the architecture of our own Colonial period.

The casement, too, has its difficulties. The inswinging type gets in the way of curtains and projects awkwardly into the room. When the window swings out, it tends to disintegrate if it is wood or rust if it is steel. The out-swinging type is most common, because it is easiest to make weathertight. Obviously, a window that closes against a frame from the outside is less likely to let rain in than one that closes from inside. However, if you want to use screens—which is something they never worried about in medieval England—you have to take the screen down to get at the window or use a mechanical operator.

The casement has two big advantages. One is that it can be opened for 100 per cent ventilation. In fact, with the offset hinges that enable the window to swing out in front of the face of the building, casements can give better than 100 per cent ventilation, as the projecting wings act like sails that scoop up passing breezes.

The next two types, which are becoming somewhat more common, are nothing more than double-hung and casement windows laid on their sides. The horizontally sliding window has the advantage of fitting into the long, low lines characteristic of the modern house. It needs no pulleys or weights, and one type on the market can be removed for easy cleaning.

The awning-type window has a casement hinge at the top instead of the side. Awning-type windows look very pretty, indeed, when banked up in a big wall of glass; they cast pleasant shadows on the exterior surfaces, and they help keep out the rain. With these windows, as with casements, there is a screening problem, because screens can only work with some type of mechanical operator.

So much for the standard types of windows. They all have one feature in common: in addition to providing a view and letting in light, they all serve as ventilators. This dual function—ventilation plus light—has been taken for granted for so long that few people think about it. But among the architects who have been re-examining every part of the house an interesting question has arisen: why do windows have to fill this dual function? The question is worth asking, because if the answer is that they don't have to, you have a freedom in handling the outside walls of your house you would never have believed possible.

Let us say, for example, that you would like to have the outside wall of one room entirely glass, and by entirely, we mean from wall to wall and from floor to ceiling. Now, if this glass screen had to be made out of windows—windows, that is, which could be opened and closed—it would be expensive, complicated to build, and also clumsy-looking, because the frames required by sash weights or hinges are thick. If, on the other hand, you accept the idea that ventilation and lighting do not necessarily have to be taken care of by the same unit, you can build a handsome, inexpensive glass wall composed of one or two big sheets of plate glass, like a shop window, or a larger number of panes of sheet glass, which costs less.

Ventilation then becomes a problem to be solved by itself. It could be done mechanically by turning on a blower which would push fresh air through registers into the room and take it out through other registers. During the winter when heat is required, this is what happens anyway.

There is another solution, however, which a few architects have found even more intriguing: the arrangement of fixed glass to let in the light and view, and smaller windows or louvers to let in the air. Combinations of movable and fixed windows are not new. The louver idea is still unfamiliar, however. Louvers can be arranged so that they look like shutters on each side of the window, or they can be installed as long, narrow slots directly underneath the sill. It doesn't matter too much how they are placed as long as they let in a sufficient volume of air to ventilate the room properly.

MORE LIGHT EQUALS LESS GLARE

The great virtue of the divided system of lighting and ventilation is that it makes possible very large windows—glass walls, in fact—without undue expense for construction or weatherproofing. It is, therefore, a device which contributes toward greater freedom in design than we have had hitherto. Whether the ventilating element is a louver, window, or door is not important: the freedom is there. But what about big windows? Have you ever heard anyone say, "It must be dreadful to live in one of those modernistic houses! Think how all that light must hurt your eyes!"

Maybe you have felt this way, too. But did you ever hear anyone say, "It must be perfectly dreadful out of doors where all that light hurts your eyes"?

The answer, of course, is not to be found in the quantity of light, but in the way in which light is used. A room with just one small window in a solid wall can be very hard on the eyes, not because there is too much light, but because the contrast between the brilliant patch of glass and the dim surroundings is almost unbearable. In such interiors, to which all of us have been exposed at one time or another, the light shoots in through the window as if from the mouth of a cannon, and its impact can be comparably unpleasant. So, strange as it may seem on first thought, the more windows a room has—always assuming that these windows have been properly distributed by a designer who knows what he is about—the softer and more pleasant the lighting will be.

It is the modern architects, and their eternal curiosity about things everyone else has taken for granted, that has brought up the whole subject of daylighting in connection with the home. As in so many other instances, they have learned what the problems and solutions are from other types of buildings, notably factories and schools. In factories daylighting is a major design factor, as it has an appreciable effect on worker efficiency, profit and loss. In schools there have been other considerations: the well-being of the pupils depends to so great an extent on adequate daylight that there are state laws which control the minimum size of windows. These laws also fix the height of the top of a window, since it has been found that light which comes in through the top of a window is far more useful than that which enters at the bottom. Light from the bottom is mostly glare while top light is soft, usable illumination. In house design this fact is important.

At the beginning of this book there were two chapters devoted almost exclusively to the problems involved in designing a living-room. Not all of the problems were dealt with, however, for we might approach the design of this room on the basis of daylighting, too.

Let us assume, therefore, that we are continuing the design of the living-room, and that the instructions given the architect demand that the lighting be so worked out that on an average day one could read or write comfortably anywhere in it. The first thing he would do would involve the creation of a window starting from a sill four or five feet from the floor, going up as close to the ceiling as possible, and extending from wall to wall. In other words, the upper half of the wall would be a window. You wouldn't like this window, and neither would the architect for that matter, because the connection between interior and garden would be

lost, and the view would be spoiled, since it could only be seen when one was standing up. In practice, therefore, the big window extends much farther down towards the floor. But this is done for considerations other than daylighting.

If the room were built at this stage of the design with a continuous high window on one side, the result would not be pleasant, because all the light would be coming in from the same direction. Shadows would be cast, and the illumination would fall off sharply as one moved away from the window wall. At the opposite wall it would drop to one-tenth its initial value, which means that the instructions given the architect would not be carried out. The next step, therefore, is to open this opposite wall, too. Now the situation is vastly improved: illumination is far more even, and the room is infinitely pleasanter. But this procedure has an important effect on the plan. Few houses have living-rooms with both long walls exposed on the outside. Usually one side has other rooms up against it. Here modern architecture can come to the rescue. The characteristic long, narrow plan with the living-room at one end can solve the problem, or, if this doesn't work out conveniently, the living-room ceiling can be raised and a band of clerestory windows installed.

A clerestory window is nothing more than a high window which occurs where roofs of differing levels come together. The old Gothic cathedrals are full of such windows in the walls between nave and aisles, and much of their atmosphere is due to this lighting device. It can be used in homes in conjunction with either pitched or flat roofs. The clerestory has many advantages: for one thing, it means that the living-room must be higher than other rooms, something most people like anyway; for another, it provides the balanced lighting we are looking for without the need to plan the room with both long walls exposed. In Taliesen, the home of Frank Lloyd Wright, there are many rooms with windows high up under the roof, and they are extraordinarily effective decoration. When the sun gets around to them, shafts of light stream through, giving the interiors a wonderfully "alive" quality owing to the changes of lighting as the sun moves across the sky.

DAYLIGHTING IS A SCIENCE

The living-room we have tentatively arrived at, with large, continuous glass areas on one side and a clerestory band on the other, is unusual in appearance compared to ordinary rooms, but it has one advantage never possessed by a conventional interior: since the light is good everywhere, furniture can be placed wherever you please. A desk or favorite easy chair does not have to be jammed up against a small window to be usable, and mother's sewing table can be next to the fireplace if she wants it there. If our living-room has little resemblance to conventional interiors, it shows an astonishing similarity to the wonderful classrooms architects have been installing in schools on the West Coast.

The problem given our hypothetical architect—provision of good reading light everywhere in the room—presents an absolute necessity in the case of schools, for desks are all over the classroom area and each child must be able to see properly. School architects began to approach the problem in much the same manner as we have discussed the living-room, and tests with light meters soon showed that the theory of balanced daylighting could be a practical reality. This is what happened in California. To the standard windows on one wall, a new set on the opposite wall was added. This new set was a high clerestory band, since there was always a corridor along one side of the room. Variations were tried. In one case, the clerestory, instead of being over an outside wall, was over the center of the classroom; this was an improvement, for it brought the light in closer to where it was needed. In another instance, the clerestory was wrapped around two walls; this helped even more. The result in these modern schools was that the standards attained by the new window arrangements were higher than those established for the best artificial lighting. Let us note here one very important point: all these architects were doing the same thing. They were scrapping the conventional window pattern in favor of a new approach based on getting the right amount of daylight exactly where it was needed. Does this sound coldly functional and completely unlivable? Parents who have seen the new California schools, and visitors to homes such as Taliesen, do not think so. As a matter of fact, they are invariably captivated by the warmth and beauty of these new interiors.

This kind of "daylight engineering"—for that is what it really amounts to—has much to offer buildings of all types, but its benefit to houses is particularly great. Think of what it would mean, for example, to have a kitchen in which all of the work surfaces, even those in the most remote corners of the room, were bright, easy to work at, and clean. Imagine what it would be like always to be able to find things in the closets without putting on a light, to step out of the house on a bright summer day without having to squint and shield your eyes for several minutes while you become accustomed to the light, to be able to see with equal ease in any part of the interior.

If houses could be built without roofs, and rooms without ceilings, these qualities would be very easy to achieve. For our homes would then be lighted by the most nearly perfect lighting surface we know anything about—the vault of the sky. This surface, which would cost hundreds of thousands of dollars to duplicate over the extent of a small factory, is capable of lighting the top of a desk or work table, shielded from direct sunlight, to a brightness of 500 to 1500 foot-candles throughout most of the day most of the year—five to fifty times the intensity produced by the best artificial lighting installations. The sky provides even, shadowless illumination from all directions, and particularly from above, where it is of the most value for seeing purposes and least objectionable from the standpoint of glare. It costs nothing to build and nothing to operate, and is available to all but the most benighted city dwellers in practically unlimited quantity.

The trouble is that whenever we build we invariably construct a lid that cuts out 80 to 90 per cent of the sky vault. We do this not only because we have to have something to keep out the snow and rain, but also because this is the only practicable shield against direct sunlight, which is far from ideal for illuminating purposes.

Fortunately, however, it is not necessary to use more than a small portion of the sky for thoroughly satisfactory lighting; as a matter of fact, a good deal less than 20 per cent will do a perfectly good job. In England, where daylight is more appreciated because there is less of it, engineers have figured out that as little as 2 per cent of the sky vault is capable of producing acceptable illumination within a room. This quantity is based on a standard of illumination described quite graphically as the "grumble point." This point is nothing more nor less than the one at which most people will get up and turn on the lights because of insufficient daylight. Obviously, when this happens about noon on a clear day, when there is every reason to expect plenty of light from the windows, you have a condition of less-than-adequate daylighting.

This is a very low standard indeed. For really good light, suitable for close work, such as sewing, it is necessary that at least 5 per cent of the whole area of the sky be visible from the point where the work is being done. This is enough to produce about twenty foot-candles of illumination at four in the afternoon on a dull December day, and about ninety foot-candles at noon in midsummer. In the average room it is the kind of light you get within a few feet of a good-sized window—pro-

vided the upper part of the window is not obstructed by a shade or curtain.

How, then, do we get this kind of lighting throughout the house, or at least wherever it is really needed? First, by raising the tops of the windows until they are flush with the ceiling, which makes a better looking window and is not hard to do with modern structural methods. Second, in large rooms, by raising the height of the ceiling itself. A good rule is that no part of the room should be more than one and a half times the height of the ceiling away from a window wall. To illustrate: if the ceiling is eight feet high, no part of the room should be more than twelve feet away from a window wall. Third, and most important, by spotting clerestory windows, skylights and other small, high openings where they are needed to light the interior portions of the house.

Naturally, good lighting cannot be the only consideration in the design of a house, and such devices must be used with skill and discretion to avoid an awkward hodgepodge of dormers and skylights. In the hands of a skilled modern architect, however, openings of this type can become real design features, inside as well as out, and frequently offer other advantages as well. A prime example of this is the type of inside kitchen which Frank Lloyd Wright has used in many of his houses, where the ceiling is raised well above the general roof line and ringed on four sides with small windows which serve as excellent exhaust ventilators in addition to letting in large quantities of diffuse overhead light. Small, high-up dormers can be used with equally good effect in living-rooms and over interior hallways; and in flat-roofed houses, perforations in the ceiling, capped by inconspicuous stock skylights for weather protection, offer similar advantages.

A few years before World War II this last device was used to produce one of the handsomest and best lighted rooms in the world: the reading-room of a library designed by Alvar Aalto, Finland's greatest architect. The ceiling of this room which is very large and very high, is perforated with scores of regularly spaced cylindrical openings deep enough to exclude the angular rays of the sun while admitting quantities of light from directly overhead. This is the only light the room receives, and it is almost ideal illumination—perfectly even throughout the whole area, completely diffuse and almost directionless, and absolutely without glare. A person lying on his back on one of the work tables would see at once that this arrangement observes the first and only rule of good daylighting: that a large percentage of the sky be visible from the point where light is needed. The ordinary visitor, however, is conscious only of the soft, all-pervading quality of the light, and the almost perfect working conditions provided.

LIGHT CONTROL

Alvar Aalto's library brings up another important daylighting problem—the need for means to control light at the openings which admit it. In the Aalto skylights control was provided by the design of the units themselves, which were ingeniously shaped to exclude direct sunlight. The same effect can also be achieved in properly oriented skylights of the familiar "north light" variety, and in clerestory and dormer windows facing in the same direction. Most windows, however, must also be used to provide outlook and let in the winter sun, and therefore require control devices of the flexible type. Even where shades or blinds are not needed to filter direct sunlight, some means must be provided for covering big areas of glass at night, both for privacy and for the sake of appearance.

The shades, curtains, and draperies which obscure the meager windows of the conventional house were originally put up in an unsuccessful and never-ending effort to overcome the effects of poor daylighting. The ordinary roller-type shade, for example, is usually pulled down to cover the upper part of the window in order to conceal the sky,

which is too bright to look at with comfort from a badly lighted room. Since this makes the room even darker, curtains are added to screen at least partially that portion of the glass which remains exposed. After the curtains come draperies, and after the draperies, over-drapes, and so on, ad infinitum. These items not only effectively shut out most of the light, but also reduce the view to a bull's eye about twelve inches square in the center of the lower part of the "window."

Modern architecture not only has no sympathy for clutter of this kind—it has no need for it. From a really well-lighted room a generous patch of sky is as comfortable and interesting a part of the view as it is from under your favorite shade tree. This, in fact, is one of the things which make such rooms so much a part of the out-of-doors: the sensation of sitting in them is so much like that of being outside. But modern windows do have a real need for flexible, easily manipulated coverings of various kinds, both outside and inside the glass. This need is best approached on a functional basis.

One of the prime functions of most such controls is to filter or exclude direct sunlight. In the chapter on solar heating we describe how permanent, external "hoods" or other projections may be used to keep the summer sun from entering large windows, but this device is at its best only on south walls and may not provide all of the control desired in late summer when the sun is low but still hot. Moreover, such projections do nothing at all to temper the glare of the winter sun, which enters at a low angle and, pleasant as it is at certain times, may be definitely objectionable at others.

In discussing the best means for controlling sunlight, it is necessary to sort out a number of threads, all of which begin at a common point but which lead in opposite directions. Controls for a south window, protected from the summer sun by an outside hood or roof overhang, are very different from those needed by a west window facing the full glare of the afternoon sun in hot weather. In the first instance, the problem is merely to diffuse and soften the *light*; in the second, what is needed is something that will completely exclude sun *heat* and at the same time permit the window to function as a ventilator.

In the case of the protected south window, inside controls such as curtains and shades (whose true function is to diffuse and filter sunlight) will do a good job, as will inside venetian blinds, which have the advantage of blocking the direct rays while reflecting a great deal of light up against the ceiling and deep into the room. In the case of the west window, outside controls such as awnings or exterior venetian blinds are needed.

In the more recently-built commercial buildings, where air-conditioning includes cooling as well as heating, engineers have discovered a very disconcerting series of facts, which hinge once again on the terrific potency of solar heat. For example, if the west side of an office building is mostly windows (and it has to be; otherwise you couldn't rent space on that side of the building), the "load" on the cooling system increases tremendously. The same is true of the south side unless projecting hoods are used, and to a smaller degree, of the east side. In other words, the nicest window found itself in the position of being the air-conditioning engineer's worst enemy, and the owner's, too, because it meant having to get rid of unwanted heat. Immediately people began wondering what could be done.

The engineers solved the whole thing very quickly and easily. "Leave out the windows," they said. And pretty soon the magazines and Sunday supplements were full of all sorts of idiotic predictions about the building of the future which would have no windows and in fact might even be built underground so that it wouldn't get in people's way while they were walking around.

In factories, to be sure, the windowless building became a reality. Many of our biggest war plants have no windows or skylights in them at all. But

here the problem is somewhat different, because in a big factory which covers dozens of acres, the workers can't look out because they are too far from the outside walls. Therefore the question of view becomes pretty academic.

The more rational solutions proposed trapping the sun before it could get through the window. This is why we mentioned exterior venetian blinds. You see, if the sun's radiant heat gets through the window, the damage is done. It doesn't matter whether there are blinds inside the window or not. The heat is already in the room and must then be disposed of by the cooling system. If the sun is trapped before it passes through the windows, then it never does get inside the room and therefore never becomes a problem.

Trapping the sun has made further changes in what we normally consider to be just a plain, ordinary window. In Brazil, for example, they have built strange and wonderful skyscrapers which on the sunny side resemble nothing so much as a huge egg crate. The north face of the building (south to us) is built not like a flat wall with windows in it, but like a waffle-shaped series of horizontal and vertical baffles. In New York City there is a town house where the windows are covered with movable horizontal fins, which do a very good job of giving light and privacy to the interiors without letting the sun in to disrupt the air-cooling system.

If the exterior blinds are made of aluminum or some other highly reflective metal, they will work particularly well, for then they will reflect the sun's heat the way a mirror reflects light, and no heat at all will be absorbed. In other words, the blinds themselves won't become warm and thus warm the air coming through them into the building.

THE GOLDFISH BOWL

So much for controlling sunlight. What about some of the other control problems? What, for instance, about controlling the neighbors? How can you have big windows and still retain a little privacy?

The answer to this question is partly a matter of planning and partly a matter of the sensible use of curtains and drapes. In the picture section which accompanies this chapter you will find a number of examples of houses in built-up areas which have used enormous glass surfaces with, if anything, even more privacy than the conventional house usually gets. There is nothing remarkable about the various ways this has been done. In one instance the architect solved the problem by building a high fence around the garden—in other words, by moving the "curtain" out to the lot line. If this seems extreme, remember that it is rarely necessary to build a wall all around the garden to accomplish the purpose. A single wall jutting out from the house at right angles to the window will usually do the trick, and at the same time provide a background for planting. Often planting alone will be enough. In some cases putting the windows in the right places (vertically as well as horizontally) will be all that is needed to avoid a "goldfish bowl" effect.

Whether or not these things are done, you will still want curtains and probably drapes to cover the window glass at night, and to take care of those times when you would like to feel a little shut in. As a matter of fact, there is nothing better looking than a really big window with a handsome, barely translucent drapery half drawn. Far from proving the big window a "failure" (as has sometimes been argued), such a use of draperies to fit the time of year and the mood of the occupants of the house serves to demonstrate one of the biggest advantages of the true window-wall: big windows are the only kind that can be made large *and* small as you see fit; small ones have to stay that way unless you want to call in a carpenter or chop away the wall yourself with an ax.

Earlier in this chapter we mentioned the use of double glass to reduce the tendency of heat to leak through ordinary windows, at a prodigious rate in comparison with modern insulated walls. Double glass reduces this heat loss by about one-half, but still leaves a lot to be desired. Here again is an opportunity for window controls to be functional as well as decorative. A good drapery, lined and interlined with heavy material, is an investment which any householder who wants large windows can well afford, since it will pay for itself in reduced fuel bills long before it wears out. Provision for draperies of this kind in the original plans of the house will permit them to be pulled entirely free of the window in the daytime and to cover all or most of the window at night, thus admitting quantities of solar heat in the daytime, and reducing heat losses substantially when the traffic is all in the other direction.

Pre-planned draperies are no novelty in modern house design and are typical of the extra care and thought which go into this type of house. Provision of "pockets" where draperies and venetian blinds can be furled so that they do not obstruct the glazed area adds little to the cost of a big window and much to the satisfaction of using it. In some cases, particularly in the case of venetian blinds which are not very handsome when pulled up overhead, such pockets are enclosed in the construction and out of sight. In others—and especially where the drapery material is a decorative element in the room—there are recesses in the wall alongside the window opening big enough to accommodate the folded material.

This sums up what we have to say about windows. They are infinitely more than a "style" feature: they can take care of some heating in winter, they can give furniture placing infinitely more freedom, they alone can provide a truly intimate relationship between garden and house, and they can combine the enjoyment of view with the enjoyment of privacy. One of the really great contributions of the modern house is its bold and generous use of glass areas.

CHAPTER FIFTEEN

SOLAR HEATING

THE STORY OF solar heating offers what is probably the best of these peculiar chains of influence which are to be seen so often in the development of the modern house. When architects in this country and Europe began to experiment with new shapes and plans and structures for buildings, one of the features which became practically universal was the big window, expanded in many instances to the point where it became a glass wall. A great many reasons were advanced for the introduction of these large glass areas. There was the fact, hard to dispute, that the view when seen through a big window is nicer than if seen through a small one. But not many houses had good views. Then there was the argument, supported by the findings of the physiologists, that less eye strain was produced in a room with glass walls than in one with just slots for windows. It was also the contention, based not on scientific fact but on an emotion shared by practically everyone, that a room flooded with sunlight was far more agreeable than a dark, dingy interior.

The architects who began building "glass houses" thirty or forty years ago had other reasons for their seemingly extravagant procedure, reasons which stemmed from purely esthetic developments all through the field of art, notably in painting. They didn't talk about these esthetic reasons to their clients because they felt—quite rightly—that if the typical homeowner were going to be sold on the idea of installing acres of plate glass in his

house, he would have to be given a good practical reason for doing so.

It was in the Germany of the Weimar Republic that modern buildings were put up in the greatest quantities and frequently in the most interesting forms. The architects of this period, which included most of the 1920's, had a theory about their glass buildings which they proceeded to put into effect. The theory sounded very good. It was that a long building, running north and south, would have its longest sides exposed to the east and west. This meant, according to the theory, that the east rooms would get sun all morning and the west rooms would get sun all afternoon.

Once built, the structures themselves punched the theory full of holes. In the first place, the cost of heating these buildings was excessive. In the second place, the cheerful morning sun varied with the seasons. In midsummer there was plenty of sunlight coming in from the east, while in midwinter, when the sun rose far to the south, there was only a short time in which these rooms received the dubious benefits of their western exposure. In the third place, people living in the west rooms found that for most of the year this exposure was practically intolerable. The interiors were blistered in summer by the late afternoon sun, and the strong light coming in at a very low angle was unpleasant and hard to screen out with shades.

The important thing about these early experimental buildings was not that they failed but that they were trying something new. They were trying to bring the house into more intimate contact with its natural environment through the use of sunlight. One result was that scientists, not architects, began to ask questions about what sunlight did do and how one should go about getting the maximum benefits from it.

THE SUN AS A HEATER

That the sun throws off a great deal of energy has been clearly understood for a long time. A physicist can tell you that the amount of solar energy which heats the earth's atmosphere adds up to about 430 horsepower per acre. This is a lot of energy. The first presentation of these facts that made sense in terms of house design came from a report published by a committee of the Royal Institute of British Architects in 1932. The British report figured out the number of hours of sunlight received each day on walls facing the different points of the compass.

Somewhat later the American Society of Heating and Ventilating Engineers carried this investigation one step further by measuring the amount of heat landing on these different walls. True, the Society was concerned with the problems of summer cooling rather than winter heating, but its work called attention to the fact that sunlight on outside walls produces substantial quantities of heat inside the room. At this point designers began to realize that they had a yardstick ready at hand by which they could compare solar heat quite accurately with the amount produced by the furnace.

Thus, barely ten years ago, a possible justification for the glass wall came into being: if somehow this solar energy could be converted into heat inside the house, there would be a way of reducing fuel bills.

The main thing revealed by the British architects' study was the reason that the east and west orientation had not worked. It was because the walls which got the most sun in winter faced neither east nor west but south. So architects began to think in terms of glass walls on the south side, and here they made a discovery so simple and so obvious that today we wonder why people didn't do something about it long before.

The problem of the house in relation to solar heating is a double one. In winter we want to let the sun's heat in and in summer we want to keep it out. Fortunately, the mechanics of the solar system make this very easy. In winter the midday sun is very low and in summer it is very high. Thus it was possible to install a permanent sun shade which projected out over a south window so that in the summertime no direct sunlight got inside the rooms. In winter the same window, with the same sun shade, was flooded with light. This solved the problem of how to admit the heat in the winter when you wanted it and how to keep it out in the summer when it only made trouble. Let us note at this point that it also changed the appearance of the house because previously it had not been normal practice to build sun shades over windows.

But new questions popped up as fast as the old ones were settled. To get the full benefit of sun on the south, this wall had to be made almost entirely of glass. In the typical Colonial house, one-sixth of the wall area, or less, contained windows. The rest was solid, and, if it was insulated to boot, this solid wall was very effective in keeping the heat in. Once the glass wall was accepted, however, it was clear enough that the system would function admirably so long as the sun was shining, for the amount of heat that got in through the glass would be much greater than that which leaked out. But what about night time and cloudy days? Here it was perfectly clear that there would be no gain and all loss, and the question to be answered was: would the balance sheet at the end of an average winter show a bigger fuel bill or a saving?

A few years ago a student at Columbia University, Henry Fagin, took precisely this theme for his graduate thesis. He considered a solid brick wall with plaster and a wall made of a single thickness of glass. He compared these walls, not to see which was the better looking or more durable or anything like that, but to find out which kind of wall would make a building cheaper to heat. Some people, when learning of this study, must have thought that he was absolutely crazy, for anyone knows that you lose less heat through a brick wall than through a single sheet of glass, which has practically no insulation value whatever.

Fagin knew this, too. But he also knew that the transmission of heat in a building is a kind of two-way street. When the sun beats on the outside walls, heat goes into the building. And when it isn't heating an outside wall, then heat leaks out. The problem Fagin set himself was to find out in which direction the traffic, so to speak, was the heaviest. Because if a glass wall let in more heat during the day than it could possibly let out during the night, there would be a net gain of heat which would be reflected in the fuel bills. Then the argument of brick versus glass would be settled.

Fagin found out that if any zone having a winter climate similar to that of New York one built a house whose south wall was entirely of glass, that house would be cheaper to heat (on a ten-year average, let us say, since some winters have more sun than others) than if there were no windows at all on the south wall, with solid brick and plaster used to keep the heat in. There are parts of the United States where this would not be true because of climatic conditions, but these parts are few and cover a surprisingly small area. One is the section which runs from the shore of Lake Erie 200 to 300 miles to the southeast. The other is the seaboard of Oregon and Washington, notorious for its persistent winter fogs. In virtually every other part of the country windows on south walls are likely to pay off.

178

The modern architects tried a new tack. "Why," they asked, "should we calculate only the heat lost through this wall of glass on the south side? Why not figure out what would happen if the plan of the whole house were modified to take full advantage of solar heating?" Here the facts of life—or rather of nature—came to the rescue. Few home builders wished to put rooms on the north side of the house if they could help it, for they knew from experience that such rooms were the least comfortable. So a shift was made in the plan: the house was stretched out so that most of the rooms would face south, and for the north side the architect reserved closets, bathrooms, stairs, and hallways—spaces which require no windows at all or fairly small ones. Thus the first step was achieved. Window sizes on the most exposed of the four walls were cut down, but without detriment to the livability of the house. On the east side windows were left at about average size, since the morning sun is pleasant all year round, but on the west side, where summer sun heat is the source of extreme discomfort, there grew up a tendency to eliminate most of the windows, or at least to shade them from the sun. The sum total of this procedure was that the house began to look like a glass house only if it were seen from one or two sides at the most, and this is why in so many of the more recent modern houses some of the views show great expanses of wall undisturbed by any windows whatever. As a final refinement in the evolution of what people have begun to call the solar house, its axis was shifted slightly to the west. By this shift the east wall gets a little more sun than it used to and so does the north wall in the summertime. When World War II broke out, there were only a few solar houses in existence that demonstrated all of these refinements. Nevertheless, a workable procedure had been established. The solar house began to receive national publicity. But it still posed many an unanswered question.

PROBLEMS AND POSSIBILITIES

Any housewife knows what the sun does to fabrics. She knows that it will make almost any color fade, that it raises the very devil with curtains, lampshades, rugs, upholstery fabrics, pictures, and even the paint on the walls. For this problem a solution has yet to be found. Part of it involves the utmost care in selecting materials whose colors are closest to being sunproof. Some of it is still waiting for the chemists, who will have to develop colors more permanent than any found hitherto. The glass companies also have a part to play in the development of special materials which will let in the sun's heat but screen out those light waves which do the most damage to synthetic and natural dyes. Some such glasses are already on the market. They have a disadvantage in that they are slightly tinted. They are usable, however, if they are placed carefully. The simplest solution, however, is probably to be found in the dyes themselves, and in judicious use of such items as venetian blinds, which will let the sun's heat get through the window while keeping the direct rays off paint and fabric.

The most interesting, perhaps, of all the possibilities of solar heating involves what we might call the reservoir principle. This can be illustrated by an example. People who live in all-wood houses of the solar type have found that they tend to become overheated while the sun is shining and to cool off almost instantly when the sun goes behind a cloud. In houses with concrete floors the reverse happens. The floors absorb much of the solar energy while the sun is shining, and it may be hours, or even all night, before the floor cools down to the point where it is no longer giving off a certain amount of heat. This happens because the massive concrete has a greater capacity than wood for absorbing and storing heat. The old fireless cooker was nothing more than a practical utilization of this simple principle.

Here, as in the case of the sun shade, we find that the sun is again influencing the design of the house in quite an unexpected way. A floor which can store the sun's heat during the day and give it off during the evening will have an effect, and a pretty important one, on the total fuel bill. But use of a concrete slab modifies the whole house plan, for it tends to force the design to one story rather than two and, incidentally, to bring the house into much closer contact with the surrounding landscape than it was before.

This, in the sketchiest possible form, is the story of solar heating. It is typical of the very best developments in modern house design because it works with nature instead of fighting it with gadgets. In the process the whole design of the house is modified. With the sun shades or overhanging eaves the house grows eyebrows, so to speak. Through the heavy concrete slab, laid directly on the ground, the outdoors and indoors are brought into closer contact with each other. Highlighting the importance of varying the amount of window area on each side of the house, gives each wall its own individual character and modifies the plan of the rooms inside for the better. From here on in, anyone who plans a house without giving serious consideration to the operation of the solar house principle is missing a wonderful chance to get a better house, a more interesting house, and a house that is cheaper to run.

CHAPTER SIXTEEN

PUTTING THE PIECES TOGETHER

SO FAR WE have approached the problems of house design through specific problems, such as planning for storage, meals, relaxation, and so on. In actuality, when a house is being designed, study of the details and the plan as a whole proceed almost simultaneously. Whatever is done to an individual space, such as a bedroom, has an effect on the spaces related to it. Until all the small ideas have been merged in a smoothly working over-all plan, there can be no house.

The plan of a house as opposed to the separate plans of its individual parts is the result of a complex process of give and take. It is rare indeed to find a house where no compromise has been made at any point along the line. Involved as this process of fitting and patching may be, however, essentially it is not particularly mysterious. Just as the design of a closet depends on how much clothing you have to put in it, so the working out of the house plan is also the result of the operation of equally comprehensible factors.

First of these is the lot itself, which may be flat or steep, regular or irregular. The successful plan will treat the house and the lot as a single unit. The lot provides the immediate view and space for outdoor living. Both must be related intimately to the house itself. Sunlight, as we have already seen, is

180

rapidly becoming an almost equally potent factor. An understanding of the benefits of solar radiation has had a tremendous influence on planning concepts, and it has begun to turn the house from a squarish box into a long and narrow one so that a maximum number of rooms can get the benefits of midday sunlight. Almost as important a factor is the direction from which the prevailing breezes come in summer and in winter.

Zoning has become a common word in our cities. To date, however, few people have tried to apply it to the house. In connection with the house, all it means is that certain major types of activities are grouped for maximum convenience and for privacy. A "zoned" house will have one or two sleeping areas, isolated as much as possible from the noisier rooms. It will have a work center, which may also be a part-time living area. It will have a service group, including heater, laundry, and possibly a portion of the kitchen; and finally it will have the general living section, which may include outside as well as inside space.

Still another factor which often forces further compromises is the point of access. At some location on the perimeter of the lot there has to be a sidewalk to the front door and a drive to the garage. Too many home builders persist in considering these separately. In today's house—and this will be even more true in tomorrow's—the entrance most frequently used is the automobile drive and not the pedestrian path. If the two can be merged and a service entrance included, planning will be immensely simplified, landscape costs will be somewhat reduced, and convenience will be enhanced.

A few decades ago the main rooms of a house were invariably placed on the street side. For this there were good reasons. Streets were relatively safe and quiet. Today the street can offer nothing more than noise, gasoline fumes, and danger, and there has been a steadily growing tendency, therefore, to reverse the old approach and put the living-rooms at the back where they could be tied in with the family's private garden.

PERIMETER VERSUS BUDGET

The most inexpensive type of medium-sized house that can be built is a cube with living-rooms downstairs and sleeping-rooms upstairs. Whenever the perimeter of this familiar plan is made larger, costs go up. It happens to be an unfortunate fact that all of the modern tendencies in house planning, such as those listed immediately above, operate to produce a house with maximum perimeter. Zoning, for example, operates more conveniently with a one-story house. So does the intimate relationship between rooms and garden, which people are coming to prefer. The long, narrow plan designed to get the most out of solar radiation also increases the perimeter of the house.

At this point there is only one thing for the home builder and his architect to do. Maximum economy must be balanced with maximum livability. You can't have both. Where cost is no consideration, there is no problem. Most of us, however, have to consider cost, and carefully. Here again you will find that compromise is probably the solution. Maybe some of the desirable features of zoning

will have to go by the boards. Maybe only two bedrooms can face south instead of all four. But every item making for greater livability should be fought for until it is obvious that the budget is nearing the breaking point.

The minimum dogma with which so many planners were infected had a short life but a hectic one. The results, however, were by no means all bad. For one thing, the open plan, with its many virtues, received a great impetus. For another, architects and builders who had been notoriously wasteful in the way they spent their customers' money began to be somewhat more practical and considerate. Nevertheless, the tendency to squeeze down the size of the house should be resisted as much as the budget will permit.

A bedroom the size of a third-class steamer cabin can be a satisfactory sleeping compartment, but a bedroom big enough to be used as a sitting-room is nice, too. A large living-room has greater flexibility and use potentialities than a small one. A separate dining-room, if you can swing it, has advantages. Small kitchens can be efficient, but we will take a large one any time we are given the choice. Small bathrooms, on the other hand, are good for very little unless they are used by one person, and there are few families which can afford the extreme luxury of one bath for each member. An adequate family bath takes a space of more than a hundred square feet, the size of a small bedroom. This is good space and it costs good money. Once again, convenience will have to be balanced against the budget.

The "space versus money" problem does not solve itself with a series of simple rules. The ingenuity of the designer can work wonders here. Take one example, a living-room. Let us say that the living-room is going to be eleven by sixteen feet. This is a small room, but perhaps no more space can be afforded. If there just happened to be a screened porch alongside the living-room and some sliding doors in the walls between, the living-room would still be eleven by sixteen but for five or more months of the year it might expand easily and cheaply to become an enclosed area of twenty by sixteen. Where space is at a premium big windows can work wonders, for these, used in conjunction with low garden walls, trellises, and other cheap exterior features, can create the impression that the space available is much larger than is actually the fact. Right here is where the topnotch architect is more than worth his fee, because he can create the illusion of additional space without making you spend the money to build it.

HOW WILL IT LOOK?

At some point in the planning process, this question arises. Rooms have been efficiently planned and carefully related to one another. The entrance is in the right place, the quiet rooms are off by themselves, the view and sunlight have been taken care of—but what is it going to look like? The conventional design approach can completely wreck a good house plan at this stage, if you let it. And preconceived notions of the proper appearance of the house seen from the outside have very little to do with a plan worked out to meet the requirements of modern living. Up to this point we have advocated compromise as a desirable, even necessary expedient. Now our advice is the reverse. Do anything but compromise. Let the house look the way it really is. If your lot is a hillside and common sense demands that you put the garage in the attic and the bedrooms two floors below, don't fret because this is a violent departure from grandmother's Colonial farmhouse. Of course it is, but you aren't grandmother. If everyone who comes to visit you arrives by car, don't make the architect shove in a front door in the center of the house just because that is the way all the other houses in the neighborhood are equipped.

Preconceived ideas are poison. It is a pretty safe rule that if a planning solution is thoroughly workable it is not going to be difficult to design an exterior which will be agreeable in appearance. It may be unconventional. Maybe the bathrooms will have big windows instead of little ones. Maybe the kitchen will be next to the front door instead of the back door. Maybe it won't even look like a house at all to those who are accustomed to symmetrical fronts with two shutters on every window. Nevertheless, in its personal, modern way, it will be a good-looking house.

For the modern architect who knows his trade, planning and design, building and site, house and family, all form a single package. The product he creates is a live thing. It fits the people for whom it was designed, it expresses the time they live in and, above all, it works, psychologically as well as physically. It does all of these things because it was conceived in a creative manner and not taken out of a copybook. Behind the finished product is a flexible, inquiring attitude. Everything in such a house makes sense. It may have walls of stainless steel or plywood, or they may be of the rough-hewn masonry used in the neighborhood for hundreds of years. For the modern architect these choices are incidental and not basic. For him there are rules but they are fundamental rules: the family and its ways of living dictate the plan, the plan determines the exterior, and the exterior responds at the same time to the latest developments of industrial technology and the most ancient of local traditions. The modern house is a good house because it is a "natural" house. Its outstanding virtue is that it is a genuine response to real needs, and its appearance has the authentic quality common to all genuine articles. If it still looks strange to you, it is only because it is still unfamiliar. But familiarity, in this case, you will find, breeds anything but contempt.

193

EXTERIORS

The outside of any house inevitably expresses the interior—even when strenuous efforts are made to avoid it. Thus conventional exteriors are expressive not only of the tight little plans that go with conventional design; they also reveal the tortured compromises this approach necessitates. And, since modern plans are freer and more imaginative, modern exteriors are freer and more imaginative in consequence. A bold conception—like the cantilevered living room projecting over the water in pictures 193 and 194—may be a determining factor; if your tastes run to less dramatic things you can expect a quieter looking result. But whatever your tastes don't expect a truly modern house to look like anything but what it is.

194

195

196

197

Back in the early Thirties, when modern architecture first began to be used in this country, the
belief was general that a building couldn't really
be modern unless it had white stucco walls and
at least one corner window. This fashion—known
to architects as the International Style—is what
most people think of when they hear the word
Modern, or "modernistic." But the modern approach has become considerably more catholic
since the days of its importation from Europe—and
incidentally, more to the liking of most people.
International Style houses are still being built,
however. Those shown here range in time from
one of the first modern houses built in the U. S.
(195) to two of the latest (199 and 200). And
for those who ask, "What would that sort of
house look like in the New England landscape?"
we have included one: 198.

198

199

200

201

202

203

204

One factor which has relieved the severity of modern architecture has been the desire to achieve a more intimate relationship with the landscape—functionally as well as aesthetically. The International Style house was frequently too detached from its surroundings: chaste and a little disdainful. In contrast, some of the more recent work is almost bawdy in the way it snuggles among the trees and against the ground. Views 201, 205 and 206 are expressive of this trend. People who hate picnics because ants get in the food may prefer a cantilevered balcony, but most of us will probably like modern better in its homier mood. And, since even the best modern house is something you will want to get out of on occasion, doing so ought to be made as easy as possible.

205

206

207

187

209

210

211

212

Architect Frank Lloyd Wright, whose masterpiece, Falling Water, is shown on the preceding two pages, went on designing contemporary houses in the years when most architects were jumping about between Cotswold, Tudor and Colonial. One of his most recent small houses is shown in 209, and a Wright-influenced design by another architect in 210. The houses on this page are examples of a distinctly different trend: a blend of American wood frame construction with the ribbon windows and structural-expressionism of European modern. The studied unconcern for outside appearance which houses 211 and 212 evidence—useful as it was in establishing an honest, experimental approach to house design—has never found acceptance outside of a limited circle of modern architects and their disciples, and is on the wane.

191

216

214

215

217

Outside appearance depends as much on the fundamental character of the house as on architectural treatment. A closely-knit, two-story house will have a solid, substantial look regardless of whether the walls are light or dark, the roof flat or pitched (216 and 217). Broad porches and spreading wings have hospitable connotations in any design idiom (214 and 215). And if you decide that a modest, story-and-a-half rectangle meets your needs you will get something that looks pretty much like an early American farmhouse. The one in 218 and 219 is actually an old farmhouse brought up to date by an architect who understood that the excellence of this building type lies not in the moldings and window muntins, but in its unpretentious approach to the problem of enclosing space.

218

219

220

221

222

223

224

Even a poor architect has a hard time making a spreading, one-story house unattractive. The best designers, working in the free style which the overthrow of traditionalism has engendered, are producing houses of well-nigh universal appeal. Depending on choice of materials and type of roof, the effect can be varied from the trim, tailored look of house 220–221 to the pleasant romanticism of 222, but both types represent a fuller exploitation of present day building techniques. Views 223 and 224, which show standardized houses from a Federal housing project, demonstrate the applicability of this approach to even the most modest sort of dwelling, provided that the details are handled with sufficient sensitivity, and view 225 shows the same vernacular carried over to a larger, two-story design.

225

226

227

228

229

230

231

The earliest modern houses all had flat roofs; anything else was considered an unpardonable concession to traditionalism. There was no compelling reason for this, however, and in later designs the gable roof reappeared, and with it a new type (new, at least, in its application to houses) known as the "shed" or "monopitch" roof. The shed roof, use of which has reached the proportions of a fad among modern designers, has much to recommend it. It is simple, easy to build, readily ventilated to keep out summer sun-heat, and good looking; moreover, it makes possible a high, open wall to the south, admitting a maximum of winter sunshine while presenting minimum wall surface to the cold winds from the north. Three of the houses shown here illustrate this design principle, 226–227, 228–229 and 231. The latter is an example of an old house remodeled along "solar" lines. View 230 shows the application of the shed roof to a small, one-room-deep design.

CHAPTER SEVENTEEN

HOW TO
GET YOUR HOUSE

(OR REMODEL THE ONE YOU HAVE)

FOR YEARS THE presses have been grinding out books and articles on how to get yourself the house you want. There are acres of printed admonitions on sound construction, how to save, where to go for a building loan, what grade of lumber to buy, and so on. We propose to deal rather lightly with these matters, partly because they have been covered so many times elsewhere, but mainly because there is a lot of hocus-pocus involved which merely serves to confuse the buyer.

Today FHA-insured mortgages and their various equivalents have been so standardized as far as technical requirements are concerned that the chances of getting a jerry-built house are fairly slim. Also, the methods of obtaining loans have been fairly well publicized, and if by any chance you have not run into this kind of information, you can get it without any difficulty from any competent architect, builder, local bank, savings & loan association, or from the local FHA office itself.

Our problem is not primarily a matter of building or financing technique. The house whose various parts and characteristics have been discussed at length is a pretty unconventional one. The approach to its planning also is not typical. Unfortunately, even if you are now convinced that this way of designing a house makes sense, there is going to be trouble.

HEADACHES FOR THE HOME BUILDER

The building industry as of this moment—or , if you like, five years from this moment—is not an industry. It is the clumsiest aggregation of builders, big and small, manufacturers, handicraftsmen, architects, and retail merchandisers one could possibly imagine. Even the conventional Cape Cod cottage, with its inevitable pair of evergreens flanking the front door and its turquoise-blue shutters with half moons cut into them, is hard to get if the house is to be a custom-built job. With the kind of house described in this book, these difficulties multiply. For one thing, a run-of-the-mill architect is not going to produce it for you. He is too enmeshed in old-fashioned drafting-room methods and prejudices to be capable of working out your problems with you on a constructive, forward-looking basis. The architects whose work appears in this book have, to be sure, already demonstrated their ability to create a superior background for modern living. But these men constitute a small group, and if all the architects in the country like them were added to the list at the back of the book, it would still be a fairly small one.

Possibly there is some young architect in your community who has ideas and can carry them out. If so, fine. Near the big cities, of course, this problem is less serious. It might be added here that there is no reason to be afraid of going to see a firm of architects simply because it has a first-class reputation. Architects as a rule have fee scales which do not vary tremendously, and many people find to their surprise that the fee charged by the best available firm is frequently no greater than that asked by its less talented competitors.

Among the better offices it is fairly standard practice to charge at least 10 per cent of the cost of a house for architectural design services and supervision. A few offices go above this figure, and some will go below. There are architects—many of them—who will set their fees at 6 per cent or even lower. These, however, do not fit into the group whose work appears here.

Perhaps you would like to know why architects have to charge a 10 per cent fee to do a decent job on a modern house. A little arithmetic should make this fairly clear. Let us assume that a house is going to cost around $12,000. This puts the architect's fee somewhere in the neighborhood of $1,200. Of this amount he will be able to recapture $300 to $400, if he is lucky, as payment for his time, which may run from three to six months or more. The remainder—say $850—has got to pay his overhead, salaries to draftsmen, and the other expenses of his business. In return for this he will camp on your doorstep, practically psychoanalyze the fam-

ily, try to distinguish what you want from what you say you want, produce a series of drawings from which the house can be satisfactorily constructed and equipped, negotiate with bidders to get the house within the budget, and arrange for changes in the plans and details. And, into the bargain, he will probably give advice on furniture, color schemes, fabrics, and landscaping, in the event that specialists in these fields are not engaged. That is why a conscientious architect cannot undertake to do a reasonably good job on a custom-built house for less than 10 per cent. Probably, if he were as good a business-man as he is a technician and artist, he would charge considerably more.

Finding a really topnotch architect, however, is only the first of the headaches, and they multiply from this point on. Whenever old-line builders are confronted with anything that deviates a hair's breadth from the way their grandfathers used to do things, they let out mighty squawks and proceed to jack up the price. They also have a disturbing habit of predicting (1) that the house will fall down; (2) that it will leak; (3) that the neighbors will lynch you; and (4) that the house could never be rented or sold.

There is another situation that has to be met. Rather early in the game your architect will find that existing home equipment, whether for lighting, storage, or some other purpose, is not properly designed, and he will suggest, frequently with good reason, that a certain amount of special work be done. This involves dealing with a miscellaneous assortment of electrical supply people, metal workers, hardware firms, and others, in an effort to concoct something superior to the stock article. Some people find that this part of the process of designing a modern house is great fun. But even so, it is a lot of work, too.

Up to this point we have been talking about some of the problems of getting the house designed and built. As it happens, there are other just as important hurdles to be surmounted. The first of these is money.

MONEY

Let us have it understood once and for all that a custom-designed and custom-built house costs more than a ready-made dwelling. There is the matter of the architect's fee, which, as we have seen, may be reasonable but is also substantial. And the architect is a "must," because there is nowhere one can write for a set of stock plans, enclosing a check for two or ten dollars. Tomorrow's house just isn't produced that way. The special equipment and fittings just mentioned will do a better job than their ready-made counterparts, but they also cost money. If you agree that a one-story house has great advantages in many instances over a two-story house, it will be found that this, too, increases the price, in spite of the fact that some savings can be made. Moreover, since the modern architect designs so that house and lot form an integral unit for indoor and outdoor living, the lot has to be reasonably generous—more so, of course, in the case of a one-story house than a dwelling with two floors.

If your budget will not permit the expenditure of extra money for extra amenities, it would be most unwise to embark on the venture of having a house designed to meet your requirements. It would be far better to buy a house ready-made because the value for a limited amount of money is greater.

YOU

The pet peeve of almost every house architect is that his client walks in and states his requirements as follows: "I want four bedrooms, two baths, a guest lavatory, maid's room, and two-car garage, and the living-room should be at least thirty-two feet long. My budget, including your fee, is $8,500.

This, obviously, is absurd. Yet everyone does it.

If one walked into an automobile showroom and said, "I am looking for a car. I must have 180 horsepower, five headlights, and a stainless steel body. My budget is $850," he would be laughed out of the place. Nobody tries this procedure with automobiles, because the product is a package at a fixed price. Today's house—and even tomorrow's house, for that matter—is not a package: it is a crazy quilt, and nobody will really know the price down to the last penny until the last bill has been paid.

The contradictory requirements of budget on the one hand and space need on the other have wrecked more potentially good houses than any other single factor. The architect, who is perennially an optimist, tries to please his client by producing a minor miracle. But this miracle, like most others, rarely comes off, and the result is a botched job with which no one is satisfied and for which everyone is blamed.

When the architect is selected and given the job, he must be given one set of limitations or another—but never both. If your budget is $8,500, say so, and he will tell you pretty quickly what you can reasonably expect to get for that amount of money at current prices. If, on the other hand, you can't live without six bedrooms and seven baths, tell him so, but don't fall into the trap of believing that you are competent to attach a price tag at the same time, because it takes even the experts a little while to figure out what the bill will probably be.

This is not an attempt to shield the architect. It is the home builder who will suffer if he refuses to take a reasonable attitude towards this all-important matter of budget procedure.

THE NEIGHBORS

Some years ago one of us designed a modern house for a Westchester suburb. Before the ground had been broken, the neighbors were up in arms. And very soon we were called to account. "What do you mean," they demanded, "by putting a modern house in our community?" (They called it modernistic.) "Don't you realize that you are destroying the homogeneity of the entire neighborhood? All of these beautiful homes will be seriously depreciated if you and your clients persist in this insane venture."

The reply to this was not very polite, but it was true. It was pointed out that the neighborhood as far as the houses were concerned was anything but homogeneous; there was an imitation French farmhouse next to a pseudo-Mediterranean villa; there were houses cribbed from work of the Georgian period in England, and there were peculiar half-timber jobs that were probably supposed to be Elizabethan.

It was also pointed out even more sharply that there was nothing that we as architects could do to the neighborhood from the architectural point of view that would make it much more chaotic than it was already. This argument was greeted with shocked silence, and by the time the irate householders could think of a reply the house was built. They thronged in for the housewarming and left a little envious, because they could see that the house was amazingly easy to live in and take care of, and that the windows were big enough to see out of and to let the sun in.

Most people who have built modern houses in the past ten years have had similar experiences, and generally the stories have ended equally happily, because whatever one's preconceived notions about the external appearance of a house, it is hard to resist the insidious charm of a well-designed modern interior.

Today the problem is not as great as it used to be. The shift in public taste in just the past few years has been phenomenal, and it is probable that in almost any community the building of a modern house would be greeted with more pleased and excited interest than with fearful disapproval. Never-

theless, this is no argument for flaunting one's eccentricities or an architect's screwball notions if the same result can be achieved in a reasonably inconspicuous way. In other words, why go out of one's way to offend the people with whom one has to live? If a house is built in a middle-western community where brick is one of the favorite materials, there is no particular reason at this stage of our technical development for not using brick. If wood is in the local tradition, or stucco or adobe or whatnot, the same holds true, because the modern house is not a rigid package to be produced only in one way and no other, but merely a reasonable and attractive framework for a family's activities.

It is particularly important to hang on to this last idea, because frequently the temptation to follow some current fad is well-nigh irresistible. It was once believed that a house was not really modern unless it was a white cube with a flat roof. Or perhaps it had to have round instead of square corners. Or maybe the "thing to do" was chromium trim smeared all over the main entrance. All this is foolishness. Modern design, it is true, does have certain characteristics which are peculiar to it. But the ones that have lasted have managed to justify themselves on a very practical basis.

THE BANKER

Your banker may not agree to this. As a trustee of other people's funds, his normally conservative tendencies have been intensified a hundredfold. Like his friend the builder, he is frequently shocked by the newfangled ideas people are getting about their houses. Colonial was good enough for his father, and it is going to be good enough for him and his son, if he has anything to say about it. This attitude is a real obstacle to surmount. It has been so great a hindrance, in fact, that most of the outstanding early modern houses were built by wealthy men who could pay for their houses without applying for a mortgage.

If your banker is recalcitrant and refuses to make a loan on the house designed for you; or, what is more likely, if he arbitrarily discounts the value of the finished house to something below its actual cost so that the mortgage is inadequate, remember that he, too, may be open to reason. And remember also that he may have competitors who are somewhat more open-minded. When World War II broke out there were already a number of lending institutions that had convinced themselves that these new types of houses were here to stay, and actually constituted a sounder investment than the conventional types, because they were less likely to get completely out of date before the mortgage had been paid off.

With existing financing arrangements for home builders, the banker is no longer quite the free agent he used to be. Most mortgages are now FHA-insured, which means that not only must the banker be convinced that the proposed house is a good investment, but so also must the regional FHA representative, who is all too often, alas, a frightened, petty-minded little bureaucrat whose only effective method for handling a difficult situation is to say "no."

In spite of these manifold difficulties, however, a lot of modern houses have been built.

THE HOUSE YOU OWN

There are almost 35,000,000 dwellings in the United States. Maybe you own one of them. If you are not entirely happy with it, ownership can be as great a hurdle between you and a new house as an overconservative banker.

To the homeowner who is intrigued by the prospects of better living offered by tomorrow's house, several possibilities are open besides the obvious one of selling the roof over his head. He can mod-

ernize its services, such as lighting, plumbing, and heating. He can add space, such as a garage storage shed or a family room. Or he can do a complete remodeling job.

Which of these alternatives to choose is one of the most perplexing problems an owner and architect can face. Costs are difficult to figure accurately, since old things must be ripped out as well as new ones installed. There is a delicate balance to be struck between the value of the house after remodeling and that of a new house which uses the proceeds of the sale of the old one. Unfortunately, there is no way in which a book can give advice to an owner confronted with a choice of this kind, because each case is specfiic and must be solved on its own. This much, however, we can say. You should not go ahead without the help of the kind of architect you would choose for a new house, and it would be wise to include a builder in the planning team. Tell them what you want, listen to the architect's suggestions, and get the builder to give his best guess on the cost.

There is another way in which this book can help anyone thinking of remodeling. The approach that has been followed throughout is one of considering living problems and workable solutions. These problems are the same in any kind of house, and most of the solutions apply equally to old and new houses. A storage wall, for example, is just as useful in a remodeled house as a new one; so are improved lighting, acoustical treatment, insulation, built-in furniture, and the other items with which we have dealt. This book, therefore, has been designed to serve as a guide to remodeling as well as planning a new home. It would be absurd to suggest that tomorrow's house could be created from a relic of the 1870's—it can't. But there is a great deal of unsuspected livability in millions of old houses that could be brought out by applying the techniques of modern planning and design.

While we are pointing out the disadvantages of

remodeling, it might be well to look at its major advantage. Designing a new house is inevitably mixed with a lot of guesswork, and no layman can possibly visualize his completed house from the lines on blueprints. As a result, seeing the house enclosed for the first time is always a surprise. Rooms are bigger or smaller than imagined. Details that had seemed very important don't count one way or the other. Almost always something has been left out or put in the wrong place. None of these things happen in a remodeling job, because you start with a complete house.

The mere process of living in a house, coupled with a reasonable amount of critical observation, produces an exceedingly intimate knowledge of its good and bad points. Planning for remodeling, therefore, is begun on a very solid and realistic basis, and for this reason, the results can be most satisfactory. There is little likelihood of wasting space or money. The owner knows which features are most objectionable, and he can insist on correcting them first. Because he knows so well those things that work badly, he will recognize proposals for improvement and understand their value. And remodeling carries a great deal of pleasure with it, not only because of the marked improvement in the house, but also because it is the one kind of building job where the layman can function on a par with the architect.

THE FUN

The difference between building an old-fashioned house and tomorrow's house is that the latter is a genuinely exciting and truly creative activity. The architect, instead of functioning as an arbiter of elegance—refusing to let you put the bathroom where it belongs because it would interfere with his symmetrical window arrangement, for instance—

becomes the leading member of a team whose sole objective is to get a house that does everything a house could possibly do. With a conventional house, planning is done within a strait-jacket. Wherever one turns there are rules which, while meaningless, are all-powerful. Windows have to have certain sizes and proportions. Materials are dictated by conditions that ceased to be important a hundred years ago. The planning is never free and the result could have been predicted in advance. With the modern house, no holds are barred. Do you want a living-room with a wall that can be slid out of the way in the summertime? You can have it. Would you prefer a screened porch without a roof on it? Your architect can make it look very handsome. Would you like to use ramps instead of stairs? Would you like to put part of the house up on stilts so that some of the garden is under cover? It has been done.

The reason that the small group of modern architects has persisted in its efforts is because they have had so much fun. They have watched their clients, skeptical at first, become wildly enthusiastic. They have seen in the completed houses how old ways of living were scrapped in favor of new and better ones. This for the conscientious professional is the highest reward he can be given.

Modern houses have been increasing in number because they sell themselves. People like the easier maintenance and the greater livability. They like the lack of clutter and the feeling of space. They like having the garden where they can enjoy it and live with it. And they tell their friends about it.

Getting tomorrow's house is a lot of trouble. We haven't pulled any punches in pointing out just how much trouble it is. But if you ever go through the headaches of building it and come out at the other end fairly unscathed, you will agree that it was worth every one of the headaches, and more.

20

CHAPTER EIGHTEEN

PROJECTIONS

UNTIL NOW we have carefully refrained from mentioning methods, techniques, and materials which are not immediately realizable in terms of today. Most houses are so far behind their potentialities that a mere listing of what has been done in a few outstanding cases can make pretty exciting reading —and these few houses have provided even more exciting living. Despite this emphasis on the practical, the temptation to indulge in crystal gazing is practically irresistible. Before embarking on our own particular dreams it might be a good idea to put a few nicks in the crystal.

A great deal of what has been written about the home of the future is hogwash. The helicopter, for instance, is a strange and wonderful thing, but at least it exists. Cars with rear engines also exist. Where the house is concerned, any overworked imagination seems to have no difficulty in getting its nonexistent products into print. The screwier the idea, the more publicity it receives.

Let us consider a few examples. We read that with the help of television mother can keep right on with the dishes while carrying on a face to face conversation with the Fuller brush man, who never gets past the front door. Any manufacturer of television equipment could undoubtedly produce this gadget, but for much less money the house can be planned with the kitchen window right next to the front door.

Consider, dear reader, the hullaballoo about the revolving house, that wondrous contraption which will turn on its foundation like a sunflower, keeping everybody tanned and happy all year long without even the trouble of pushing a button. This, too, could be built, but we have already seen that the house that doesn't revolve can be pretty well designed to take care of the sun in the southern quadrant, which is the only time it is much good anyway.

Then there is the mobile house, that wonderful package which can be unhooked from the lot when you have a quarrel with your neighbor, put on wheels, and trundled to a happier neighborhood. Mobile houses can be built, too. In fact, they have been. But what is the worth to you in dollars and cents of something you would not use more than once in twenty years?

The list of idiocies brought forth by the pseudo-scientific writers is legion. Apparently they believe that the American public will swallow anything as long as the label of novelty is attached to it. Right at the moment there is a good bit of talk about window glass being replaced by sheets of clear plastic, a little rumor that has driven a number of reputable manufacturers practically out of their minds. The facts are (1) that glass is a plastic (and has been for generations); (2) it makes very good windows and is relatively inexpensive; (3) there is no other known plastic at any price that has the unique resistance of glass to abrasion. Bomber noses are made out of plastics, to be sure, but they cost a small fortune and have to be reconditioned every few flights. Plastics are used on planes because they are light and easily formed, but no house has ever presented air-combat requirements. There are enough wonderful things coming along to satisfy any of us. If we must indulge in daydreaming—and we all like to—let's approach tomorrow's house on a more reasonable basis.

A pretty good beginning is with equipment. If one takes the trouble to look into the history of apparatus for the home, one or two facts stick out prominently. Most significant is a steady reduction in bulk. In your grandfather's house the furnace was a sheet metal octopus, a huge belly with fat tin tentacles reaching all through the cellar, poking their way up through the floors into the walls. Today's warm air furnace is a quarter of its size and does twice as good a job. The same is true of the stove, and of the refrigerator, half of which used to be an ice compartment. This trend can and will continue. With radiant heating, for example, radiators and registers have been reduced to the vanishing point. But radiant heating still uses a lot of pipes. When electricity gets to be our most common fuel, the pipes may well disappear along with the furnace. Before this really revolutionary development takes place, however, heating equipment now being designed promises to reduce the furnace to the size of a steamer trunk or a suitcase.

Reduction of bulk is important because it saves space and makes maintenance easier. Closets are a good example. In our own time we have shifted from separate wardrobes and other pieces of movable storage furniture to compact built-in closets and storage walls. In the future storage will unquestionably be almost 100 per cent integrated with the house. Furniture manufacturers may not like this prospect but we suspect housewives will.

As important as reduction of bulk is flexibility of control. To go back to heating for a moment, the old hot air furnace pumped a lot of heat into a lot of rooms. Some were too hot, others were too

206

cold; all were drafty. Equipment already on the market has eliminated most of these annoyances and we can count on further refinements. If you wanted an air-conditioning system for your home which would give individual temperature control for every room in the house, you could have it, but it would cost a lot of money. Our guess is that in the not too distant future you will be able to have it, and it won't cost a lot of money.

One of the questions we are asked most frequently by starry-eyed prospective home builders is, "What about those wonderful new materials that are being developed? When will we be able to get them for our house?" There are two answers to this. One is that there are a lot of wonderful old materials. Take that middle-western favorite, for example, a wood frame wall with an exterior finish of brick. It is a phenomenally good wall. The outside keeps its trim appearance indefinitely. The inside can be thoroughly insulated. Anybody can build it. Does it disillusion you to have the house of tomorrow discussed in such terms. Let us say that a manufacturer is trying to develop new exterior facing material. Here is what he has to produce: a material that will retain its initial good appearance indefinitely; requires no maintenance; keeps out the weather; does not shrink or warp noticeably; is strong enough to resist mechanical injury—that is, it can't fall apart if some overenthusiastic youngster bangs it with a baseball bat; and is relatively inexpensive. If it satisfies these conditions and offers into the bargain the advantages of light weight and quick installation, we have a new material that will compete effectively with the old. Anybody who produces this material has a rich and wonderful market waiting for him. Unquestionably it will be produced and ultimately accepted—but no one knows how soon. To do our own crystal gazing, let us take a look at the house as it is and as it might become.

The house is the only important consumer product which is still assembled by craftsmen. Practically every dwelling in the United States consists of sticks of various lengths called studs, floor joists, and roof rafters, put together out in the open in all kinds of weather by people who use tools going straight back to Neolithic times. This is going to change—and drastically. It is going to change because the home market is too big for industry to pass up. Once production engineers start figuring out ways to give more product for less money, things are going to happen. You don't have to be a minor prophet to guess what these things are. Even the least technical-minded among us has a fairly clear idea of how the process works.

HOW INDUSTRY FUNCTIONS

The manufacturer's dream is an operation that is automatic from beginning to end. The raw metal comes in at one end and the finished product comes out at the other. In the middle are a lot of machines which cut, press, squeeze, stretch, turn, or punch. The machines are very big and very expensive. They can be afforded only if what they turn out is produced in quantity and without flaws. To be sure, there are all kinds of manufacturers. Some make wrist watches with movements the size of a dime, and others make locomotives. It seems reasonable to assume that industries making large assemblies give us the best clue as to what will happen to the house, which must be a series of large assemblies. Three such are the automotive, aviation, and ship-building industries, and all offer interesting examples. When a car manufacturer wants to make a roof, he doesn't put up a lot of rafters, cover them with sheeting, and lay a lot of shingles on top. He has a series of big presses which squeeze out each roof in one operation. He can eliminate the rafters because he is playing on one of the most significant characteristics of sheet metals. Sheet metals left flat are weak. Curved, crimped, or corrugated, they are tremendously

strong. You can prove this to your own satisfaction with a cardboard shirt stiffener. Stood on edge, this piece of heavy paper can't even hold itself up. Twist it into a tube and it could probably support a set of the *Encyclopaedia Brittanica* plus a couple of telephone books. A car fender is far more complicated than a cardboard tube, and it is much stronger, because the simple curve has been formed into a compound curve. Houses built of sticks and stones are the carpenter's and mason's delight, but once they start coming out of factories it will be a different story.

We can count on the following: (1) More and more houses in the years to come are going to be factory-produced; (2) they will be built of sheet materials, used not only for finish inside and out but for their structural qualities as well; (3) because sheet materials function most effectively in curved rather than flat forms, the house of the future may look very strange. Do you like the idea of a corrugated kitchen or a circular bedroom or rooms without square corners anywhere in them? Most of us would have to get rid of a lot of preconceived notions before we accepted anything but our favorite rectangular shapes, but it might not be so hard. The pride of many a Colonial mansion is an elliptical stair hall. During the late years of the French Renaissance there were circular boudoirs and anterooms. The Eskimo, too, would probably consider it strange if he had suddenly to go and live in a house that was all square corners. Nobody kicked when cars went from square corners to curves. Tastes can be very deep-rooted, but tastes can change.

THE INDUSTRIALLY PRODUCED HOUSE

The machine-produced house we label "prefabricated" has caused a considerable amount of argument. People like to believe that their homes are individual, even if the facts of life show that they very rarely are. Mrs. A and Mrs. Z have already

Far-fetched

gone on record against prefabrication because they fear that the monotony would be intolerable and a mass-produced house would lack the charms of home. What gives a home its charm is not necessarily special tailoring, but the process of living in it. We have all seen apartments and third-hand houses which are full of charm and individuality—the result of what their occupants did to them. In other words, almost any personality can be imprinted on any dwelling. There is also this point: mass production, oddly enough, makes for less monotony rather than more. When nails were made by the local blacksmith, each nail was slightly different from all the others—but there were few types. Today there are hundreds more kinds of nails, although their production is highly standardized. If this is true of so completely simple an item, it must certainly hold for the house.

Prefabrication today is anything but an established industry. Yet already there are types and methods which promise a tremendous variety of finished products. Some houses are being built in panels, others are constructed in chunks, like trailers. Materials include wood, plywood, asbestos, reinforced concrete, insulating board, and sheet steel. New ideas on design and construction appear almost daily. The facts strongly suggest that whatever industrial production does to the house, it will not destroy the variety everyone demands.

DESIGN FOR TOMORROW'S LIVING

Within our own lifetime we have watched servants disappear and mechanical aids come in. We have seen women go first into offices and then into factories. We have gradually watched a general shifting of the center of gravity from the home to the community. These are broad social and economic trends which will continue. Houses are going to reflect them. Anything that pays out in the way of labor-saving design has a good chance of acceptance. Survivals, no matter how much we are at-

208

tached to them, will go by the boards. Take the case of carpets. A good carpet costs more than a good floor. Even in a home of modest means, carpets and rugs may represent an investment of a good many hundred dollars over a period of twenty or thirty years. Why do we have carpets? We started having carpets because our feudal ancestors found life on cold stone floors intolerable without some insulating material laid over them. This is no problem any more. We also have rugs because a room without them sounds queer. In other words, it is our practice to put acoustical material on the floor in the home rather than on the ceiling as in offices. This could be changed. To date, there is no single material which combines the advantages of a rug—that is, its softness, sound-deadening and decorative qualities—with the advantages of a structural floor. Such a material, however, is not too far off. It has to be resilient, easily cleaned, warm in appearance, and not more expensive than the carpets it will replace. Are you appalled by the idea of a house without rugs? The chances are about five to one that your grandchildren will be appalled to learn that you ever had such unsanitary contraptions in your house.

HORSEPOWER

One of the interesting by-products of World War II is the tremendous number and variety of fractional horsepower motors that have been turned out in a great hurry. The B-29, for example, uses well over a hundred of these little gadgets. The house of the future may not use a hundred, but it will probably use quite a few. Walls that open to the out-of-doors, such as the huge sliding windows seen in many modern living-rooms, might as well be motorized as not. The same goes for partitions, whether between children's bedrooms, the living-room and dining-room, or dining-room and kitchen. A push of the button and the wall isn't there any more. Portions of roofs could be operated in

gadgets

the same manner. Awnings or outside blinds could be operated by motor, using photo-electric cells activated by the sun so that you would not even have to push a button. All of these amenities are technically feasible now.

If you counted the number of motors in your house right now, you would probably be very impressed. There are the fans, the refrigerator, washing machine, ironer, sewing machine, oil burner, maybe the garage doors, and probably five or six others. Horsepower has already invaded the home. All we are suggesting is that the front may presently be widened.

MORE MATERIALS

World War II produced more than fractional horsepower motors. It developed the paper-laminated plastics, which are as strong, weight for weight, as aluminum. It produced wood that doesn't swell or shrink. It created plywoods which have extraordinary strength and water-proof qualities. It took aluminum out of the class of an almost rare metal and made it, with magnesium, one of the most common. It expanded stainless steel production to the point where at least one manufacturer has been talking about using stainless steel for roofing. This, incidentally, would be an exceedingly good idea because the reflecting qualities of stainless steel would do a lot toward keeping the house comfortable in the summertime. Its mirror-like surface would reflect solar radiation in much the same manner as aluminum foil insulation, but it would have the additional advantage of considerable strength.

One company developed cases for shells, using a sandwich of plywood and metal. Precut at the factory, these cases could be shipped flat, assembled by merely folding the pieces into boxes. The metal covering served as a hinge, a principle that might well be taken over for closets, cupboards, and other storage units. Another type of plywood has a strong paper surface, which can be furnished

in any color or pattern. Glass has moved out of the kitchen to serve for piping, insulation, and fabrics, and it is being combined with rayon and plastics to create new materials. Water pipes of flexible plastics may be standard in homes tomorrow, and lights without wired connections have already been demonstrated. There is a process by which soft woods are made as hard as ebony and maple. Old and new materials are emerging in a bewildering variety of forms and combinations.

Lest our enthusiasm for these novel materials run away with us, let's try to remember this: to the householder it doesn't make a great deal of difference whether his water comes out of pipes of plastic or of brass. He will never know the difference if his walls are insulated with glass or with some older type of material. These developments, while technically interesting, only mean something when they have a direct relationship to better living.

THE CRYSTAL BALL

Using industrial techniques in other fields as a basis, we think tomorrow's house will be built in pieces in factories and assembled at the site. It may be full of all sorts of queer curves, strange slanting walls, and odd materials that absorb sound but can be cleaned off with a hose. Its windows will not be single sheets of glass but insulated sandwiches with two or even three panes in a single frame, whose surfaces may be treated, as photographic lenses are now treated, so that reflections are entirely eliminated. This could be very pleasant. Imagine being able to look out of the living-room window at night without seeing reflections of lamps and furniture. Under such conditions a view might really become something to be enjoyed.

Tomorrow's house will be highly mechanized. Its present supply of fractional horsepower motors will be multiplied by two or three, and all sorts of things will happen at the push of a button instead of the heave of a back. Electricity may become the prime fuel as well as source of power. Bathrooms will probably be prefabricated and may have their own instantaneous electric hot water heaters. Individual room air-conditioning is certainly in the picture, but instead of bulky ducts to the separate rooms there may be small pipes through which the air will pass at a high velocity.

Many things will completely disappear from view in the house that is now shaping up. Bureaus and chests will give way to built-in cupboards. Radios will move from pretentious oversized cabinets into the walls. A good deal of furniture for sitting will tend to become an integral part of the walls. This creates the prospect of a series of flexible, uncluttered interiors where there is room to swing a cat and where there may be less need to swing a mop. Possibly you like cluttered interiors. This is all right, too, because our little crystal ball tells us that there will be no law in 194X compelling you to give up your Duncan Phyfe highboy and chintz curtains.

Most of us react to change in a pretty standard way. When the tractor replaced the horse, romantics pined because they liked the picture of a team of horses on the brow of a hill at sunset, a stalwart farmer urging on his tired steeds. But every time a farmer got money enough for a down payment on a tractor he bought one. Maybe farmers don't have fun any more. In the absence of proof we are inclined to doubt it.

A home in the days of our childhood was loaded to the brim with all kinds of strange and wonderful junk. There were whatnots full of sea shells, attics loaded with musty trunks, glass chimes on the front porch, stuffed animals on the mantelpiece, and all the rest of it. Maybe the youngsters are going to miss a lot of fun in tomorrow's house. But maybe that is what was said about yesterday's house, too. Deep inside Africa and Australia there are tribes that have never even seen a house, and, if the anthropologists are to be believed, even these

people have had some good times in their quiet way. It is unlikely that tomorrow's house is going to be so devoid of enrichment and interest that the youngest generation will be in the same spot as its contemporaries in darkest Africa. It is unlikely, too, that as long as people are people their houses will fail to give them whatever it is they demand.

For our part we can see a pretty good time in this newfangled piece of industrial shelter which is already beginning to appear. If it is quieter, easier to take care of, better to live in than its predecessor, it is doing just about everything a family can demand of a house.

TOMORROW'S HOUSE IS HERE

The reason we indulged in the pleasant game of projecting trends was to prove that the potentialities of tomorrow's house are very much with us today. There are materials yet to be made, and machines to be made simpler and less expensive, and production techniques to produce more space for less money. There will undoubtedly be revolutionary developments in lighting, heating, and the other services of the home. Tomorrow's house in this sense will never come all in one neat cellophane package. It will grow, item by item, year by year. With what we now know about planning and materials, and what architects have learned from the industrial and commercial fields, the house that can be built right now is a pretty wonderful thing. Every age has produced the amenities it wanted the most. This was as true in the days of Queen Victoria as it will be fifty years from now. Today is no exception.

The real fun of building tomorrow's house today comes from the time lag. Almost all of our dwellings, even the new ones, are ten to fifty years behind what they could be. If you want individuality, and that means if you really want it and just don't give lip service to the idea, this is the way to get it, and the time to start planning is right now.

210

ARCHITECTS AND DESIGNERS
WHOSE WORK APPEARS IN THIS BOOK

CALIFORNIA

Clark & Frey, 869 North Palm Canyon Drive, Palm Springs: 199

Hervey Parke Clark, 210 Post Street, San Francisco: 188, 189, 204, 215

Frederick L. R. Confer, R. F. D. #1, Box 415A, Martinez: 176, 203

Mario Corbett, 210 Post Street, San Francisco: 27, 225

Robert Trask Cox, 1570 Poppy Peak Drive, Pasadena: 205

Gardner A. Dailey, 210 Post Street, San Francisco: 20, 158, 212, 222

J. R. Davidson, 1417 Comstock Avenue, Los Angeles: 161

John Ekin Dinwiddie, Architect; Albert Henry Hill, Associate, 233 Sansome Street, San Francisco: 14, 38, 138

Joseph Esherick, Jr., Ross: 121

Willard Hall Francis, 1539 Bentley Avenue, West Los Angeles: 57

John Funk, 21 Columbus Avenue, San Francisco: 172

Michael Goodman, 2422 Cedar Street, Berkeley: 90, 91, 211

Harwell Hamilton Harris, 2311 Fellowship Parkway, Los Angeles: 58, 59, 61, 80, 101, 115, 120, 126, 131, 155, 165, 166, 175, 210

Philip Joseph, San Francisco: 38, 138

George Kosmak, Ruth Gerth & Associates, 1226 Sutter Street, San Francisco: 110, 114, 134, 137, 226, 227

Paul Laszlo, 362 North Rodeo Drive, Beverly Hills: 31, 32, 35, 73, 157, 174

Francis E. Lloyd, 210 Post Street, San Francisco: 13, 149, 153

Clarence W. W. Mayhew, 330 Hampton Road, Piedmont: 71, 164

Richard J. Neutra, 2300 Silverlake Boulevard, Los Angeles: 62, 103, 140, 169, 170, 197

Emrich Nicholson & Douglas Maier, Los Angeles: 201

W. L. Pereira, 519 North Crescent Drive, Beverly Hills: 216

Raphael S. Soriano, 6731 Leland Way, Los Angeles: 102

Lloyd Wright, 858 North Doheny Drive, Los Angeles: 19, 206

William Wilson Wurster, Wurster & Bernardi, 402 Jackson Street, San Francisco: 68, 69, 159, 160, 162, 163, 220, 221

COLORADO

Burnham Hoyt, 400 Colorado National Bank Building, Denver: 127

CONNECTICUT

Richard M. Bennett, School of Fine Arts, Yale University, New Haven: 21, 190

Thorne Sherwood, Mayapple Road, Stamford: 30, 218, 219

DELAWARE

Victorine and Samuel Homsey, Hockessin: 152

DISTRICT OF COLUMBIA

George Howe, Supervising Architect, Public Buildings Administration, Federal Works Agency, Washington: 39, 40, 193, 194

A. Musgrave Hyde, New York: 130

Philip Johnson, New York: 171, 173

Morris Ketchum, Jr., 5 East 57th Street, New York: 113

William Lescaze, 211 East 48th Street, New York: 123, 145

John Manzer, 220 East 41st Street, New York: 60, 217

Moore & Hutchins, 11 East 44th Street, New York: 56, 67

George Nelson, 4 East 95th Street, New York: 4, 6, 16, 43, 50, 78, 104, 105, 150, 151

Pomerance & Breines, 18 East 48th Street, New York: 47, 202

Antonin Raymond, 101 Park Avenue, New York: 10, 141

Jedd Stow Reisner, 26 East 55th Street, New York: 113

George Sakier, 9 East 57th Street, New York: 98

Morris B. Sanders, 219 East 49th Street, New York: 18

Walter Sanders, New York: 54, 55, 116

Willard B. Smith, 1929 E. Genesee Street, Syracuse: 99, 146

Theodore Smith-Miller, 235 East 72nd Street, New York: 54, 55, 116

Eldredge Snyder, New York: 207

Edward D. Stone, New York: 48, 89, 108, 112, 124, 129, 177, 178, 179, 180, 187, 195, 196, 223, 224

van der Gracht & Kilham, 101 Park Avenue, New York: 135, 136

Paul Lester Wiener (formerly Contempora, Inc.), 33 West 42nd Street, New York: 118

Virginia Williams, New York: 145

Henry Wright, 48–13 39th Avenue, Long Island City: 21, 72, 150, 151, 167, 168, 190, 192, 228, 229, 231

NORTH CAROLINA

Allen J. Maxwell, Borden Building, Goldsboro: 223, 224

John J. Rowland, 330 North Queen Street, Kinston: 223, 224

OHIO

H. Creston Doner, Director of Department of Design, Libbey-Owens-Ford Glass Company, Toledo: 93, 94

Ernst Payer of Rideout & Payer, Chagrin Falls: 226, 227

PENNSYLVANIA

Robert M. Brown, Philadelphia: 119

George Daub, 2123 Delancey Place, Philadelphia: 125

Kenneth Day, Miquon: 12, 100, 154

TEXAS

Alden B. Dow, Inc., Houston: 5, 25

WASHINGTON

Paul Thiry, 468 Stuart Building, Seattle: 81, 82, 144, 156

WISCONSIN

Frank Lloyd Wright, Taliesin, Spring Green: 44, 45, 75, 186, 208, 209

PHOTOGRAPHERS WHOSE
PICTURES APPEAR IN THIS BOOK